Avoiding Corporate Breakdowns

Avoiding Corporate Breakdowns

The Nature and Extent of Managerial Responsibility

LaRue Hosmer

and

Patrick J. Barry

First published in 2013 by
PALGRAVE MACMILLAN®
in the United States—a division of St. Martin's Press LLC,
175 Fifth Avenue, New York, NY 10010.

Where this book is distributed in the UK, Europe and the rest of the world,
this is by Palgrave Macmillan, a division of Macmillan Publishers Limited,
registered in England, company number 785998, of Houndmills,
Basingstoke, Hampshire RG21 6XS.

Palgrave Macmillan is the global academic imprint of the above companies
and has companies and representatives throughout the world.

Palgrave® and Macmillan® are registered trademarks in the United States,
the United Kingdom, Europe and other countries.

ISBN: 978–1–137–32290–6 (pbk)
ISBN: 978–1–137–32291–3 (hc)

Library of Congress Cataloging-in-Publication Data is available from the
Library of Congress.

A catalogue record of the book is available from the British Library.

Design by Newgen Imaging Systems (P) Ltd., Chennai, India.

First edition: April 2013

10 9 8 7 6 5 4 3 2 1

Contents

Figures

Preface

What is managerial responsibility? Perhaps at its most basic level, it is the duty to understand, and attempt to avoid, the harmful impacts of managerial decisions and actions upon the person making the decision, the organization at which he/she is employed, and the society of which he/she is a member. These wide-ranging harmful impacts are becoming much larger in scope and more frequent in occurrence, and require—in our view—changes in the nature (to whom) and the extent (for what) of managerial responsibility. Let us give just three examples of these events, each of which we believe truly deserves the term "corporate breakdown."

Blowout, Explosion, and Fire On Board the Deepwater Horizon

Two very large companies, British Petroleum and Transocean Corporation, together with four smaller and more specialized firms in 2008 formed what is termed a "horizontal joint venture" (multiple companies working on the same project at the same time and—in this case—at the same location) to cooperatively drill for oil in what had previously been the unexplored outer reaches of the Gulf of Mexico. This was known to be a complex and difficult undertaking. The ocean at the drilling site was slightly more than one mile deep, while the anticipated petroleum reserve, or "pay zone" that had been located through ultrasonic soundings, was four miles further down, far beneath the ocean floor. The pressures and the problems from that immense weight of sea water and crumbling sedimentary rock were of a magnitude that had never been encountered before.

The *Deepwater Horizon* had been specifically designed to deal with those pressures and those problems. It was the largest and most technologically advanced drilling platform that had ever been constructed, with automated processing controls, redundant safety components, and specially trained crew members. A widespread feeling soon developed both on board the drilling rig and on shore at corporate offices that a highly destructive blowout, explosion, and fire simply could no longer occur. However, managers at many of those different companies made decisions and took actions that directly benefited their own firms, and thus indirectly themselves, but increased the collective risks for the full joint venture and—as it turned out—for the full society. The result in 2010 was the largest blowout, explosion, fire, and uncontrolled oil spill in American history, with catastrophic impacts not just upon the participating companies but also upon the regional environment, economy, and society.

Collapse of the Residential Housing and Mortgage Securitization Industries in the United States

Literally hundreds of companies, small, medium, and large, formed in the late 1990s what is termed a "vertical value chain" (multiple companies working on the same project at sequential times and at different places) to cooperatively first construct the homes and then finance the sales of residential housing to middle- and lower-income families. These families, mostly hard working and in large measure possessing decent credit histories when this venture began, had up to this point been deemed ineligible for home mortgages because they lacked the savings required for what was considered to be an industry standard 20 percent down payment. A group of innovative mortgage lenders, however, argued that the rapidly rising prices of newly purchased homes would soon supply, after just a few years, the owner's equity that was thought to be needed to ensure mortgage payments, and thus down payments ceased being a requirement. The rising prices, the available mortgages, and the eager buyers created an economic boom across the United States in residential housing that lasted for slightly over six years.

There were six steps or levels within this residential housing value chain from tract builders to home buyers to mortgage lenders to securitizing banks to rating agencies to the eventual security purchasers. Market prices for the mortgaged homes kept rising, which continually increased the demand for new homes and for new mortgages. It was widely felt that nothing could go wrong with this market-driven value chain based upon what were thought to be solid property values and reliable property owners. However, managers at some of the companies within some of those steps or levels made decisions and took actions that benefited directly their own firms, and thus indirectly themselves, but increased the collective risks for the full value chain and—once again, as it turned out—for the full society. The result, starting in 2006, was the most severe economic downturn since the Great Depression of the 1930s, with catastrophic impacts not only upon the participants in the value chain but also upon many individuals, groups, and organizations outside that chain. By 2008, the total recorded amount of mortgage-backed securities issued and sold between 2001 and 2006 had reached $13.5 trillion, and much of that securitized debt had "improper ratings, incredible complexity and problematic value."[1]

Lead Poisoning of Preschool Children within the United States and Western Europe

For at least a century prior to 1990, the products of the early childhood toy industry were generic; that is, if you had seen one stuffed bear, wooden locomotive, or cast car you had seen them all. They were typically designed and manufactured by family-owned companies in the United States and Western Europe, and sold through local toy stores. But then, soon after 1990, a new market entrant entered this tradition-based industry. These were the marketing specialist firms. They changed everything.

These marketing specialist firms contracted with the large media companies for the rights to produce simple stuffed and wooden toys based upon popular book and TV characters such as Winnie the Pooh, Big Bird, Bob the Builder, and Thomas the Tank Engine. They then arranged for the production of these toys through low-cost manufacturers overseas, primarily in China, and for the containerized shipment of the toys directly to the warehouses of the "big box" retailers in the United States and Western Europe. This was a high-volume, high-margin vertical value chain that was highly successful, but there was one large though unrecognized problem.

This large though unrecognized problem was brought about by the dominant firms at each end of the value chain: the media companies and the big box retailers. They held the pricing power because without their agreement nothing could happen. As old contracts expired or new toys were developed, they demanded price concessions from the marketing specialists. The marketing specialist firms passed those price concessions along to the Chinese manufacturers, and suddenly everyone within the value chain was enjoying rising sales and growing profits except for one group: the Chinese manufacturers. They had the same rising sales but far narrower, almost non-existent, profit margins. They responded by replacing the contract specified acrylic finishes with lead-based paints. Lead-based paints were not only far less costly to purchase than the contract specified acrylic finishes, but also much easier to apply.

Lead paint can be exceeding harmful to preschool children, even in the minute amounts that come from the habit—familiar to all parents—of continually licking their fingers while playing with toys or other objects. The brains and bodies of preschool children are in very rapid development at this age level and lead has a scientifically proven propensity to affect that mental and physical development. The Consumer Product Safety Commission heard of the use of lead paint in 2007, tested a few toys, and promptly ordered RC2 Corporation (one of the major marketing specialist firm) to recall one and a half million Thomas and Friends train sets, and Mattel (another major marketing specialist firm) to recall one million assorted wooden and metal toys.

It is impossible to accurately estimate the financial cost of this tragedy because the mental and physical impact of the absorbed lead upon the minds and bodies of the preschool children who played with those 2.5 million toys can never be fully known. The mental acuity and the physical coordination of the children can be measured but unless there happened to have been earlier "base line" tests of those capabilities for those children the debilitating impact of the ingested lead upon that acuity and that coordination could never be accurately determined. And, of course, a dollar figure is meaningless when it concerns long-lasting impacts upon the mental and physical health of preschool children. The true costs here are the emotional agonies of the parents and the life prospects of the children, and those cannot be converted into meaningful financial equivalents through any realistic means with which we are familiar.

We assume that most readers will readily agree that all three of these very unfortunate but very different events that have been described above were massive corporate breakdowns. They differed on the impact dimensions: financial, environmental, social, medical, emotional, reputational, et cetera. They differed on the financial consequences: market declines, clean-up costs, taxpayer bailouts, regulatory fines, civil judgments, injury claims, et cetera. They differed on the social outcomes which, though immeasurable, may have been the most severe of all. But, we believe that there was one factor on which there probably were absolutely no differences at all. Everyone involved, both those who were negatively impacted and those whose decisions and actions appear to have brought about those negative impacts and their financial, environmental, social, medical, et cetera consequences, sincerely wish that these events had never happened.

The topic of this book is how to prevent the corporate breakdowns that have so very severely impacted so very many people, both those who were involved in the original decision or action, and those who were not.

Before moving on in the text to a discussion of the complex causes of those breakdowns and an explanation of the basic changes we recommend to prevent them, we should like to express our grateful appreciation to McGraw-Hill/Irwin for permission to use a limited number of diagrams, definitions, and portions of manuscript that had previously appeared in LaRue Hosmer, *The Ethics of Management: A Multi-Disciplinary Approach*, 7th edition, McGraw-Hill/Irwin, 2011. We do appreciate their kindness.

CHAPTER 1

Defining the Problem

The crew members, engineering supervisors, and contractor specialists on board the Deepwater Horizon must have felt both pleased and proud on the morning of April 20, 2010. They had successfully completed drilling what BP (formerly British Petroleum) termed the Macondo well to a near-record depth. The "wellhead" (the partially embedded top structure of the well, where the valves, controls, and emergency disconnects were located) was on the ocean floor, 5,000' beneath the surface of the sea, and the "pay zone" (the large reservoir of oil and natural gas that had been reached) was 20,800' further down, past numerous layers of hard sedimentary but easily fragmented rock. Everyone involved, both those on board the drilling rig and those on shore in company offices, recognized that this was a remarkable achievement.

> At 8:52 a.m. [during the morning of April 20, 2010] Daniel Morel [BP's head engineering supervisor on board the Deepwater Horizon] e-mailed the Houston office to reiterate "Just wanted everyone to know the cement job went well. Pressures stayed low, but we had full returns on the entire job. We should be coming out of the hole shortly". At 10:14 a.m. David Sims, BP's new operations manager in charge of the Macondo well, e-mailed to say, "Great job, guys!"[1]

The Deepwater Horizon was the oil-drilling platform that had made this achievement possible. It was huge, complex, and expensive. It weighed nearly 35,000 tons, only slightly less than a World War II battleship, but unlike the battleships of that era that were built for speed, firepower, and armored protection, the Deepwater Horizon had been constructed for stability, precision, and operational efficiency. Think for a moment about the design challenges those three essential characteristics imposed. Each time that a drill bit became dull while grinding though the sedimentary rock strata of the site and had to be replaced, it was necessary to pull 5 miles of 6″ diameter steel drill pipe out of the well, through the wellhead, up to the surface, and then to the top of the 200′ tall lifting derrick where it was disassembled into 90′ sections and then stacked vertically, ready for reassembling and relowering into the well after the new drill bit had been attached, and this all had to be done while the drill platform was held stable, not rocking back and forth due to wind and wave pressures (which would cause the drill pipe to swing dangerously) nor drifting off even slightly from its chartered position (which would greatly complicate reentry into the well hole). The top of the wellhead on the ocean floor had an opening 52″ in diameter, and the drilling crew had to thread their descending 40″ diameter drill bit through that opening from one mile above, in the total darkness of the deep ocean, relying on underwater lights and electronic cameras for guidance, and those lights and cameras had to be designed to withstand the weight of a vertical mile of ocean water pressing upon their weakest components.

How was all this accomplished? Innovation, automation, and computerization. The Deepwater Horizon bore no relation whatsoever to an anchored ship. It consisted of four rectangular steel decks that were held 50′ above the surface of the sea by four equally large steel columns, one at each corner of those decks, that in turn rested upon two massive steel pontoons that were semi-submerged, their tops just barely above the surface of the sea. The four decks were above the impact of all except the strongest waves, and provided the enclosed spaces that were needed to house the power units, the communication systems, the control processors, the command centers, the drilling inventories, the fuel supplies, and the crew quarters, dining facilities, and relaxation areas that made the two-week tours of 12-hour shifts on board this drilling platform endurable if not enjoyable.

The top or "drill" deck of the Deepwater Horizon was open, and held the 200′ tall lifting derrick, the 100′ tall pipe stacking rack, and the raised helicopter landing pad that was needed for shore to rig and rig to shore travel. Boats were O.K. to bring supplies but not to bring personnel who were, in large measure, trained, experienced, and expensive.

The two massive steel pontoons that supported the four steel columns, the four steel decks, and all of the heavy machinery and supplies needed for drilling operations had been positioned just slightly above the surface of the sea to reduce the wave impacts. These pontoons had been designed with curvilinear bows that could be pointed into the wind to further lower the impact of those waves. Water could also be automatically pumped back and forth between lengthwise compartments within each pontoon, and between the pontoons themselves, to help stabilize the structure and reduce rocking.

Positioning of this huge and awkward structure directly above the drill head was accomplished by large power thrusters (essentially hydraulically driven variable-speed enclosed propellers with automatic adjustment for the propeller-blade speed and the propeller-blade pitch) to continually point the drill platform into the prevailing winds and waves. These thrusters were powerful enough to resist winds and waves of gale force. This entire positioning system—thrusters and controls—responded to a dynamic global positioning methodology that maintained the location of the Deepwater Horizon directly over the wellhead.

This structurally large, technologically complex, and financially expensive drilling platform was owned by Transocean, a petroleum industry servicing firm that specialized in deepwater exploration around the world. Transocean also supplied two crews of about 80 persons each for the alternating two-week tours. These crews still had a few of the traditional roustabouts who did the hard labor that has always been a part of oil-field exploration and production with a certain "get out of our way and we'll get the job done" swagger, but in large measure they consisted of employees who had been personally selected by Transocean for their extensive experience in shallow-water drilling operations and then technically trained by Transocean in the rapidly changing machines and methods needed for deepwater drilling. There was a general feeling throughout the industry that these Transocean employees, particularly the senior foremen, knew what they were doing.

In addition to the 80 Transocean employees who were on board the Deepwater Horizon on the morning of April 20, 2010, there were also 5 BP supervisors, all petroleum engineers, who had participated in the design of the well, and now set goals and parameters for the drilling operations following that design, and approved changes in those operations as problems or obstacles (rock strata that was harder to drill than expected, or looser and more easily fractured than wanted) were encountered. There were even further a number of technical specialists on board who worked for other oil industry servicing firms (Schlumberger, Halliburton, Baker Hughes, et cetera) that had developed new methods, materials, and techniques for deepwater drilling. These specialists were either present on site to assist and advise in the use of those methods, materials, and techniques, or they were brought out on special trips by helicopter for that purpose.

The Deepwater Horizon was drilling for oil in a section of the Gulf of Mexico in which BP owned the exclusive drilling rights, but the technically advanced drilling platform was owned by a different firm, the technically trained crew was supplied by that company, and many if not most of the technically complex services were provided under contract by still other companies. Of the approximately 230 persons on board the Deepwater Horizon on the morning of April 20, 2010 (including a 40-person group provided by a still different contractor that attended to the cafeteria, cleaning, and laundry needs of those on board), only five were directly employed by BP.

This "contract out, don't hire in" strategy had in the past worked very well for BP. They took the discovery risks in the deepwater exploration for oil, but they did not bear the fixed costs of having the needed equipment and essential skills in-house, ready for use when needed, or cover the start-up costs for the research and development of the new and needed equipment. This outsourcing for deepwater drilling equipment and technically advanced skills started in the 1990s, and became dominant during the 2000s:

[Following the wave of oil industry mergers in the late 1990s] management pared away overlapping functions and laid off employees, reinforcing the trend towards outsourcing R&D and reducing internal technological expertise.[2]

A new generation of drilling platforms coming on the market [in the early 2000s], along with advances in drilling technology, encouraged BP to take the risk to explore [deepwater] prospects. Outpacing most of the industry by a year, the company shifted its sights [to those deepwater regions]. Rich rewards followed with a historic string of rich oil finds.[3]

This BP trend toward outsourcing R&D and reducing internal technological expertise did not seem to have affected operations on board the Deepwater Horizon. Despite the obvious authority divide between the BP engineers and the Transocean drillers, and despite the traditional competence divide between those with technical education and those with workplace experience, there seemed to have been few conflicts or disputes over the drilling methods. Perhaps this was because everyone understood that they were doing something new and difficult, and that it was necessary to work jointly and not argue individually to get things done.

In addition to the apparent spirit of cooperation and acceptance that brought together the Transocean crew members, the BP engineering supervisors, and the outside contractor specialists, there doubtless also was an underlying recognition that things could get very bad very fast if mistakes were made. This had happened frequently enough in the past on other drilling rigs operating out on the Gulf of Mexico to make everyone aboard the Deepwater Horizon fully conscious of their personal risks:

> Drilling for oil has always been hard, dirty, dangerous work, combining heavy machinery and volatile hydrocarbons extracted at high pressure. Since 2001 the Gulf of Mexico workforce—working on 90 big drilling rigs [though few others as large, complex, and efficient as the Deepwater Horizon] and 3,500 production platforms—had suffered 1,550 injuries, 60 deaths and 948 fires and explosions.[4]

Lastly, there was without question a widespread awareness that the Macondo oil well was six weeks behind schedule and $58 million over budget.[5] Probably few people on board the drilling rig talked much about this matter, but in most companies this sort of issue is brought up more than occasionally in dispatches from district offices and memos from corporate headquarters. It can easily be understood that everybody on board much preferred to put that particular aspect of their performance record behind them, given that the exploration phase had finally been so successfully completed. Now they doubtless felt that it was necessary to focus on preparing the Macondo well for conversion to the production function as quickly and inexpensively but safely as possible.

We have attempted, in the previous few paragraphs, to propose a set of the probable goals, norms, beliefs, and values that guided the decisions and actions of the various supervisors, drillers, and contractors who were working jointly on board the Deepwater Horizon during this conversion stage. These goals, norms, beliefs, and values varied by individual, of course. There was no universally accepted set, but *together they doubtless formed the informal way that things got done for this job on this drilling platform at this time.*

We have emphasized this last statement because we believe that the behavioral patterns that develop over time in the performance of complex tasks for difficult projects or programs where the responsibility is shared by multiple organizations are often the neglected factor in the follow-up analyses when things go terribly wrong. Our argument is very simple. People who are working actively together for the successful completion of a large and complex project or program but are employed by different corporations and have different job skills, different knowledge bases, different experience levels, different risk perceptions, different performance measures, and different incentive systems *will almost inevitably develop a common pattern of cooperation and acceptance with which they jointly feel comfortable.*

By "acceptance" we mean a general feeling of "Well, I may not really like what you are doing, or plan to do, but you probably know more about this part of the work than I do, and if I object it will just put us further behind, so go ahead." We believe that the decisions and actions that were taken during the temporary closure of the Macondo well will illustrate this alleged pattern of "get the job done now and don't argue about it until later" cooperative acceptance.

This temporary closure of the Macondo well was required so that the Deepwater Horizon could be disconnected from the current wellhead and moved to its next drilling assignment. It would be replaced on this site by a much smaller and less complex production platform that would connect the wellhead to an undersea pipeline, reopen the well, and supervise transferring the oil and natural gas from the deepwater reserve to an onshore refinery for processing, storage, and sale.

Closing a deepwater oil well is not an easy task. The problem is the immense pressure of the oil and gas held within the newly discovered reserve. The pressure is much greater in deepwater wells than in shallow-water wells because both the ocean depth and the well depth are much greater. The problems of this pressure, and the difficulties of controlling it during drilling operations, were clearly described in a section of the report prepared by the National Commission on the BP Deepwater Horizon Oil Spill and Deepwater Drilling:

> The principle challenge in deepwater drilling is to drill a path to the hydrocarbon filled pay zone in a manner that simultaneously controls those enormous pressures and avoids fracturing the geologic formation in which the reservoir is found. It is a delicate balance. The drillers

must balance the reservoir pressures pushing hydrocarbons into the well with counter pressure from inside the wellbore. If too much counter pressure is used the formation can be fractured [permitting the hydrocarbons to escape, which leaves the reserve depleted and the environment polluted]. If too little counter pressure is used, the result can be an uncontrolled intrusion of hydrocarbons into the well, and a discharge from the well itself as the oil and gas rush up and out of the well. An uncontrolled discharge is termed a blowout.[6]

The term "blowout" barely describes the event or the consequences. Natural gas within a deepwater pay zone has been compressed by the weight of the overlying rock layers and sea water into a liquid form. Once released into the drill pipe or the well casing without control, it becomes a gas, expands rapidly in volume, and pushes all of the other hydrocarbon fluids toward the surface with increasing velocity. Natural gas is highly flammable and the accompanying crude oil, usually in droplet form as a result of the rapid acceleration of the mass, will readily sustain a conflagration. The result of an uncontrolled blowout can only be described as catastrophic.

Avoiding this catastrophic event during the temporary closing and production preparation of a deepwater well is more difficult than during the drilling of that same well. During drilling, there are three paths for the highly pressurized hydrocarbons within the pay zone to escape into the well bore and up to the wellhead: (a) outside the well casing, (b) inside the well casing, or (c) inside the drill pipe. (All of these terms will be more fully described in the next section of this chapter). During drilling, the first of those paths—outside the well casing—is periodically sealed with cement after the sequential sections of that casing are installed. This is termed the "outer cement seal." The other two paths—inside the well casing and inside the drill pipe—have the constantly monitored counterforce brought about by the weight of the four-mile columns of heavy drilling mud in those paths.

During the closure process, a new path is introduced. This is the "riser pipe" that is designed to carry the oil and natural gas from the pay zone up to the wellhead. The riser pipe is inserted inside the well casing, but outside the drill pipe. During the next-to-the-last stage of sealing, cement is pumped down the well pipe to first seal the space between the casing and the riser, and then to seal the end of the riser, all at the bottom of the well. These two seals are termed "bottom cement" plugs. After those two cement plugs are set in place, the entire well structure—between the well bore and the well casing, between the well casing and the riser pipe, between the riser pipe and the drill pipe, and inside the drill pipe—is tested to ensure that all four of those paths have been securely sealed and blocked from any possible escape of the highly pressurized hydrocarbons within the pay zone.

After the successful completion of those tests, the drill pipe is withdrawn about halfway up the riser pipe. This is the start of the final stage in the closure process that the senior BP supervising engineer on board the Deepwater Horizon had earlier described, in an email previously cited from National Commission on the BP Deepwater Horizon Oil Spill report, as "coming out of the hole."[7] In this last stage, the counterbalancing drilling mud in the riser pipe has to be replaced with sea water (cement sets much more firmly in sea water than in drilling mud) and a final or "safety cement" plug is then installed. If the earlier, bottom cement plugs set in drilling mud did not hold, then the safety cement plug set in sea water should block the onrushing oil and natural gas in the riser pipe. If that failed, then reliance would fall upon the emergency shutoffs in the blowout preventer, mounted at the wellhead.

With four levels of protection—outer cement, bottom cement, safety cement, and shutoff valves in the blowout preventer, and with backup power sources and control systems for those shutoffs in that preventer—it was widely believed throughout the industry that a blowout during a professionally planned closure of a deepwater oil well simply could not happen. But, this did happen at the Macondo well, within ten hours of that confident "we're coming out of the hole" email. The resulting explosion and fire sank the Deepwater Horizon, killed 11 workers on board that drilling platform, injured many others, and released 5 million barrels of toxic crude oil into the Gulf of Mexico, badly damaging the quality of the local environment and severely harming the livelihood and lives of the area residents.

The balance of this chapter will attempt to describe: (a) the mechanical structure of a deepwater oil well so that the steps in the closure process can be better understood; (b) the standard steps in the closure process of a deepwater oil well; (c) the early reactions—confused but at the same time courageous—by the engineers, drillers, and contractors on board the Deepwater Horizon in response to the blowout; (d) the specific choices during the closure of the Macondo well that apparently led to that blowout; (e) the troubling questions raised by those specific choices during the closing of the Macondo well; and (f) the behavioral issues underlying those troubling questions that—let us repeat—we believe to be the critical but neglected causes of the disastrous outcomes that seem to occur so frequently not only in deepwater drilling but throughout our highly competitive and increasingly complex economy, society, and government. Now, on to the mechanical structure of a deepwater oil well.

The Mechanical Structure of a Deepwater Oil Well

The mechanical structure of a deepwater oil well, from the wellhead on the ocean floor to what is called the "shoe end" in the pay zone, is a combination of time-tested parts, specially prepared compounds, and highly sophisticated equipment. The time-tested parts are the drill pipes, well casings, and riser pipes used in similar form at oil wells throughout the world on both land and at sea. The specialty compounds are the muds and cements that must be continually modified to adjust to the pressure, temperature, chemical, and geological conditions as those are encountered at each well during both drilling and closing. The highly sophisticated equipment is all contained in the blowout preventer, that is: (a) mounted on the wellhead; (b) controlled from the command center on the drilling platform; and (c) maintained one mile deep in the ocean by what is essentially an unmanned robotic submarine with arms, hands, and tools.

1. *Drill pipes*: The drill pipe consists of heavy steel tubes, usually with a 4″ inside diameter and a 1/2″ wall, that come in 30′ sections that are connected together with threaded steel joints. The threaded joint connectors are also heavy steel tubing, with a 5″ inside diameter and a 1/2″ wall, each 12″ long. The drill pipe rotates within the well bore, and both turns the drilling bit at the bottom of the well and conveys the drilling mud that lubricates and cools that drilling bit. The drill pipe also conveys the sealing cement when needed both at specific stages during the drilling and then finally for the critical stages at the end.

2. *Well casings*: The well casings are lighter steel conduits, rolled from steel sheets rather than pierced from steel bars, that are used to line the well bore. The well bore, as can well be imagined, is the rough hole that has been left by the drill bit as it works its way through hard but flaky sedimentary rock. In order to prevent both the accidental cave in of loose sand and gravel layers encountered during the drilling process or the unintended flow of oil and gas from the porous rock formations passed by the drilling process into the well bore, that bore

has to be lined with the well casings. These come in 20′ sections that are joined together by welding on the top deck of the drilling platform while held vertically over the well by the drill derrick, and then lowered incrementally (i.e., after each new section has been added, the entire string is lowered another 20′) into the well bore. After a 1,000′ to 1,200′ string has been lowered, then the entire string is cemented in place, both to prevent the escape of hydrocarbons outside the well casing and to support the weight of that casing string. Cement is pumped down the drill pipe and forced up to fill the space between the casing string and the well bore.

It can readily be understood that once the first string of well casings, perhaps with an outside diameter of 48″ and a 3/16″ wall, has been cemented in place, then the next string has to be smaller, probably with an outside diameter of 46″ and the same wall thickness. An oil well that was 4 miles deep, as was the Macondo well, would require a minimum of 16 diameter decreases. These figures were not revealed in the National Commission report, but it can be assumed that 48″ was the starting point and 16″ the last section. This accordion structure of the well casings had a definite impact upon the decisions and actions taken during the well closure process.

3. *Drilling mud*: Drilling mud is a blend of petrochemical liquids, fine-grained clay, and assorted chemical compounds. The clay particles are the weighting agents. The percentage of those particles suspended in the column of mud within the well bore provides the counterforce needed to block the escape of any highly pressurized oil and natural gas reserves encountered during drilling, and then at the completion of drilling, from the pay zone. This column of petrochemical fluids and clay particles, termed "mud" for the obvious reason, has to be both heavy enough to create an adequate counterpressure to block the escape of the oil and natural gas from the pay zone into the well bore, and at the same time light enough so as not to overcome the pressure of the oil and natural gas within that pay zone and force its way into the reserve. Overly dense drilling mud can fracture the structure of a reserve, permitting the escape of valued hydrocarbons into the overlying porous rock layers and eventually into the sea.

The drilling mud is pumped under pressure through the drill pipe to first cool and lubricate the drill bit and then to carry the drilling residue back to the surface through the well casing to the wellhead and then further up to the drill deck where the rock slivers and sand bits from the drill bit are filtered out before the mud is recycled back down to the drill bit at the bottom of the well bore.

4. *Drilling cement:* Drilling cement is used primarily during the drilling process to fill the void between the outer surface of the steel well casings and the inner surface of the rock well bore. Filling this void with highly adhesive cement is important for two reasons: (a) the cement blocks the flow of any pressurized oil and natural gas accidently encountered during drilling up the outside of the well casings to the wellhead where it might escape into the sea; and (b) the cement attaches the steel well casings to the rock wall of the well bore to provide support for those casings. The full casing string, from the wellhead to the pay zone, in a deepwater well such as the Macondo, is over four miles long and clearly needs solid support.

   This drilling cement must be specially formulated to adjust to the temperature and pressure conditions within the well bore and to the chemical composition of the drilling mud. Cement sets less firmly in drilling mud than in sea water due to the petrochemical fluids that provide the liquidity to the mud. These specially formulated cement mixtures are almost always prepared by contractor specialists. Halliburton was the cement contractor specialist for the Macondo well, and which generally had at least one employee on board the drilling platform to help in both the mixing and pumping operations.

5. *Blowout preventers*: A blowout preventer (BOP) is a huge, 4 story tall, 400 ton mechanical device that is bolted to the top of the wellhead, which in turn had been bolted to the top of the well casings that had been cemented in place over the full length of the well. It was widely believed that, with this sequence of solid attachments firmly in place, even the extreme pressures of a blowout could not dislodge a blowout preventer.

   All of the pipes, casings, tools, and compounds (mud and cement) used in drilling the well had to pass through this solidly anchored blowout preventer on their way down to the drill face, and all of the oil and gas hydrocarbons encountered during drilling operations and all of the mud liquids recycled from those drilling operations had to pass through this unit on their way back up to the surface. It was also widely believed that, if the well casings had been solidly cemented in place, a blowout could not bypass the blowout preventer. It would have to come through that preventer and, as the name implies, there were multiple systems in place to prevent exactly that.

There were hydraulically operated hatches, valves, and controls for all of the "pass-through" openings within the blowout preventer. And, there were "fail safe" backups as well. The preventer was equipped with thick rubber gaskets that, when activated, would squeeze tightly around the central drill pipe that conveyed the drilling mud and cement down to the drill face and thus would stop the flow of any hydrocarbon liquids or gases that had, despite the counterpressure of the drilling mud and the protection of the cemented casings, entered the "annular," or the space between the drill pipe and those casings. In addition, if any hydrocarbon liquids or gases entered the drill pipe, the preventer was also equipped with giant steel shears that, again when activated, would cut through the drill pipe and form a solid steel barrier to any liquids or gases coming up that pipe. Reserve power sources and "dead man" controls had been installed so that in the event that all power lines (electric or hydraulic) and control circuits from the drilling rig on the surface to the blowout preventer on the ocean floor were damaged or disconnected, the rubber annular ram and the steel pipe shear would automatically close. Again, it was widely believed that a blowout, even of the strongest size, could not get through the internal safeguards of a blowout preventer.

Standard Steps in the Closure of an Oil Well

The temporary closure of the Macondo oil well had been scheduled so that the Deepwater Horizon exploration platform could be disconnected from the existing wellhead and moved to a new drilling assignment. It would eventually be replaced at the Macondo site by a much smaller and less expensive production platform. Workers on that production platform would then connect the wellhead on the ocean floor to an undersea pipeline, test that connection, remove the cement plugs that had blocked the pressurized oil and natural gas from escaping during the moving and connecting processes, and then supervise the flow of the oil and natural gas from the pay zone to an onshore tank storage facility and—eventually—to a refinery. This temporary closure process was well known, and normally took place in a series of standard steps.

1. *Installation of a riser pipe:* The riser pipe is a steel tube that is installed during closure to convey the oil and natural gas from the newly discovered pay zone up to the wellhead, for eventual connection to the undersea pipeline. There were two accepted forms for the riser pipe.

The first riser form was termed a "multi-string." This was very similar to the well casing, and was designed to fit fairly snugly within that well casing that, as described earlier, gradually decreased in outside diameter. This form of riser pipe was rolled from steel sheet in 20′ sections that had an outside diameter that was perhaps 2″ less than the well casing within which the section was to fit, and then those sections were welded together and incrementally lowered into the well, held vertically during this welding and lowering process by the drill derrick. When a 1,000′ or 1,200′ string had been lowered—the same length as the encircling well casing—it was cemented in place, and then another string, perhaps 2″ smaller in outside diameter to fit within the next well casing, was welded, lowered, and cemented. The final riser string, usually about 8″ in diameter, reached beyond the encircling well casing, well into the pay zone.

The second riser form was termed a "long string." This was far simpler than the multi-string type. It too consisted of 20′ sections that were fabricated from steel sheet, and then those sections were welded together and incrementally lower into the well, held vertically during this welding and lowering process by the drill derrick, exactly as the multi-string form. The difference was in the diameter. The long string, from the wellhead to the pay zone was all 8″ in diameter. The riser sections were less expensive to purchase, and they could be installed more easily and quickly, but they were more difficult to cement in place because there was a much wider space between the riser and the surrounding casing that had to be solidly filled with cement.

2. *Bottom cement*: The next step was the formation of a cement barrier or plug at the lower ends of both the newly installed riser pipe and the encircling well casing structure to prevent any unauthorized entrance of the highly pressurized oil and natural gas from the hydrocarbon reserve into either that riser pipe or that well casing. This was felt to be the crucial step in the closure process. Halliburton was the company that had formulated the cement to match the temperature, pressure, and chemical conditions encountered during drilling to seal and support the outer well casings, and they were also to formulate the cement needed for these bottom cement seals.

The cement was to be pumped down the drill pipe, which remained centered within the newly installed riser pipe, and out the end of that riser pipe that had been extended into the pay zone, beyond the protective well casing. This would be a very delicate operation. The cement had to be pumped at a pressure high enough to overcome the counter-pressure of the oil and natural gas within the pay zone, but not at a pressure high enough to force its way into that pay zone. This difference, particularly narrow at the Macondo well due to an easily fractured rock structure within the pay zone, was termed the "cement margin." That is, the pressure had to be high enough to flow out of the end of the drill pipe and up along the space between the riser and the drill bore and eventually into the bottom 500′ of the encircling well casing, but not so high as to force its way into the pay zone. If the latter happened not only would some of the reserves be lost through fracture of the rock structure within the pay zone, but also the bottom seal could be incomplete, and susceptible to a blowout. And, all this had to be done with no means for visual inspection, four miles further down below the wellhead on the ocean floor.

The volume of cement to fill those voids—the well bore space around the unprotected riser and the first 500″ of the protective well casings—was first calculated and then mixed and pumped into the drill pipe. When that amount of cement was in the drill pipe, more drilling mud under pressure was used to force the cement through that pipe and into its proper position. After that cement was in place, and had time to set, the integrity testing of the almost completed closure process could be started.

3. *Integrity testing:* "Integrity," in oil field parlance, refers to the total isolation of the basic oil-well structure—the space outside the well casings, the space inside the well casing but outside the riser pipe, and the space inside the riser pipe—from the pressurized oil and natural gas reserves within the pay zone. Testing for the soundness of the bottom cement plugs that were formed to seal off those three spaces was done with two different pressure tests: positive and negative.

For the positive pressure test, the drilling crew members conducting the test first made certain that the well casing, the riser pipe, and the drill pipe were all filled with drilling mud so there could be no compressible air that might affect the test results. They then increased the pressure on that mud to considerably above the upper limit of the drilling margin. This was the pressure at which the drilling mud within the well would have been expected to easily overcome the counterpressure of the oil and nature gas within the pay zone, and forcefully enter that pay zone. But now, the path to the pay zone had been blocked by the recently installed cement plugs so that no liquids from within the well structure should have been able to reach that zone despite the pressure increase. Once the target limit of the drilling mud pressure increase had been reached, the pump was turned off. If the drilling mud pressure remained exactly the same, then that was considered evidence that there was no leakage outward through the cement seals, and thus that these closure seals were solidly in place. That was the result here, and so the positive pressure test of well integrity of the Macondo well was declared to have been successful.

For the negative pressure test, the drilling crew members conducting the test reduced the pressure on the drilling mud within the full structure of the well to considerably below the lower limit of the drilling margin. This was the pressure at which the highly pressuring oil and natural gas within the pay zone would have been expected, if there were any weak spots in the cement seals, to force its way into the well casing, riser pipe, or drill pipe of the well and result in a pressure increase. Here there was a problem. The pressure quickly began building up, indicating evidence that there was leakage inward through those cement seals.

The drilling crew, all of whom had extensive experience in offshore drilling, was confused. Apparently, there was no leakage outward through the cement seals but there was considerable leakage inward through those same seals. There was a lengthy discussion, and eventually the shift foreman explained that he had encountered this situation once before. The cause was something he called the "balloon effect," and it came from a leakage of one of the many pipes that came down to the wellhead from the drilling platform into the wellhead, not from the pay zone into the well bottom. The solution, he continued, was to conduct another negative pressure test with the pressure changes measured in an input pipe, not in the drill pipe. This time the input pipe reduction in pressure did hold, though the drill pipe pressure continued to show an increase, but this was felt to confirm the balloon effect stressed by the drill foreman and so the negative pressure test of the Macondo well integrity was also declared to have been successfully completed.

4. *Safety plug:* Following what was said to have been the successful positive and negative testing of the bottom cement plugs, the drilling crew then began pumping the drilling mud back up from the riser pipe to the top deck on the drilling platform where it was screened to take out any rock and cement shreds and then sent to a storage tank. The drilling mud was

replaced by sea water that was admitted through a valve on the blowout preventer. Sea water is lower in density than the drilling mud so it stayed on the top. The intent was to draw the drilling mud down below the 3,000′ mark within the riser, where a second or "safety" cement plug was to be formed. Cement sets much more solidly in sea water than in drilling mud, and that was the reason for the draw down of the drilling mud for the safety seal. This was to be the final step in the closure process, but this safety seal or plug was never put in place. Without the counterpressure of the drilling mud in the top third of the riser, the oil and natural gas from the huge reserve in the pay zone pushed into that riser pipe, probably through a defect or channel in one of the bottom cement seals, and began rushing up toward the wellhead. If the blowout preventer did not hold, a full-scale blowout was now inevitable. The blowout preventer did not hold and, as everyone now knows, a very full-scale blowout did occur.

Early Reactions to the Blowout, Explosion, and Fire

At about 9:30 in the evening of April 20, as he was preparing to retire for the night, Randy Ezell, the senior foreman in charge of drilling operations onboard the Deepwater Horizon, called Jason Anderson, the foreman of the night shift who had just completed the negative pressure test and was now drawing down the drilling mud in preparation for the installation of the safety cement plug. The following conversation took place:

> *Ezell*: "How did your negative test go?"
> *Anderson*: "It went good. We bled it off. We watched it for 30 minutes and we had no flow" [of the oil and natural gas trapped within the pay zone into the well bore].
> *Ezell*: "What about your displacement?" [replacing the drilling mud inside the riser with sea water so that the safety cement plug could be installed].
> *Anderson*: "It's going fine."[8]

Less than an hour later, while Ezell was watching TV in his cabin, his phone rang. It was Steve Curtis calling, the #2 man on the drill deck and assistant to Jason Anderson. This time the news was horrifying:

> *Curtis*: "We have a situation. The well is blown out. We have mud going to the crown" [the top of the drilling derrick, 20 stories above the drilling deck on the Deepwater Horizon].

Ezell: "Do y'all have it shut in?"

Curtis: "Jason is shutting it in now...Randy, we need your help."

Ezell: "Steve, I'll be...I'll be right there."

He [Randy Ezell] put on his overalls, pulled up his socks, and started across the hall to his office, to get his boots and hard hat. Once in the hall [he later remembered] "a tremendous explosion blew me probably 20 feet against a bulkhead, against the wall in that office. And I remember then that the lights went out, power went out. I could hear everything deathly calm."[9]

The calm did not last for long. Micah Sandel, the gantry crane operator whose cab was on the open drill deck, took up the testimony at the National Commission on the BP Deepwater Horizon Oil Spill hearing:

I seen mud shooting all the way up to the derrick...Then it just stopped...I took a deep breath thinking that "Oh, they go it under control". Then all the sudden the mud started coming out the degasser [a processing unit designed to separate and flare off any highly combustionable natural gas that came up the well bore along with sea water or drilling mud] so strong and so loud that it just filled up the whole back deck with a gassy cloud. Loud enough...it's like taking an air hose and sticking it in your ear. Then something exploded. That started the first fire...on the starboard side of the derrick. Everything in the back just exploded at one time. It knocked me to the back of the cab. I fell to the floor....put my hands over my head and I just said, "No, God, no". Because I thought that was it.[10]

It was either "it" or close to "it" for many of the crew members of the Deepwater Horizon. Douglas Brown, the chief mechanic of the rig, was in his cabin next to the engine room. He could hear the diesel engines revving up in speed, running out of control. They were pulling in natural gas through their air intakes, and no longer responding to their automated throttles.

The power went out. Seconds later an explosion ripped through the pitch-black control room hurling him against the control panel, blasting away the floor. Brown fell through into a subfloor full of cable trays and wires. A second huge explosion roared through, collapsing the ceiling on him. All around in the dark he could hear people screaming and crying for help.[11]

There was certainly plenty of courage in response to the blowout, explosion, and fire. Randy Ezell, the senior foreman whose actions were described earlier, stumbled out of his cabin and found Wayman Wheeler lying injured in the passageway, covered with debris. Randy helped him to his feet and started to carry him toward the lifeboat deck.

> *Wheeler*: "Set me down". "Y'all go on. Save yourself."
> *Ezell*: "No. We're not going to leave you. We're not going to leave you in here."[12]

There was also plenty of confusion resulting from the blowout, explosion, and fire. Steve Bertone, the chief BP engineering supervisor on board the Deepwater Horizon, was at his emergency station on the bridge, along with Jimmy Harrell, the senior Transocean drilling manager, Daun Winslow, a senior BP operations manager visiting from the Houston office, and a number of other dazed and in many instances injured individuals from those two firms. Steve Bertone saw Christopher Pleasant, one of the BP engineering supervisors, standing next to the panel with the emergency disconnect switch (EDS) to the blowout preventer. Activating that switch should operate the giant pipe shears within that preventer and totally close off the riser and drill pipes to any further flow of the spouting oil and natural gas.

> Bertone hollered to Pleasant, "Have you EDSed?"
> Pleasant replied he needed permission. Bertone asked Winslow [the senior BP operations officer visiting from Houston] was it ok and Winslow said yes.
> Somebody on the bridge yelled, "He cannot EDS without the OIM's [the "offshore installation manager's"] approval.
> Harrell [the senior Transocean drilling manager who was technically the OIM because he was "on board," not "from shore"], still dazed, somewhat blinded and deafened, had also made it to the bridge... With the rig still latched to the Macondo well, Harrell was in charge. Bertone yelled, "Can we EDS?" and Harrell yelled back, "Yes, EDS, EDS."
> Pleasant opened the clear door covering the panel and pushed the button.
> *Bertone*: "I need confirmation that we've EDSed."
> *Pleasant*: "Yes, we've EDSed.
> *Bertone*: "Chris, I need confirmation again. Have we EDSed?"
> *Pleasant*: "Yes."[13]

Something was drastically wrong with either the EDS switch on the bridge of the Deepwater Horizon, with the power pipes and control cables that stretched from that drilling platform down to the blowout preventer on the ocean floor, or with the close-off rams and shutoff shears mounted on that preventer because the flow of oil and natural gas did not stop. Instead, as explained earlier, it continued unabated and eventually destroyed the Deepwater Horizon and severely damaged the Gulf of Mexico's environment and economy.

Specific Choices in the Closure of the Macondo Oil Well

What went wrong? Why did this disastrous event occur? This was the result of a series of specific choice that occurred both before and during the closure of the Macondo well. We will list those choices in the chronological order in which they occurred:

1. *Purchase of the blowout preventer*: Blowout preventers can be built with either one or two sets of the giant steel shears that are designed to cut through the steel drill pipe and form a solid block to any pressurized oil or natural gas coming up that pipe. Two sets were preferred because the shears could not cut through the drill pipe *and* the threaded connectors that joined those pipes sections. Each pipe section was 30' long and each pipe connector was 1' long so that, if there were only one set of pipe shears in the preventer there was a 3.33 percentage chance that the shears would encounter a connector and fail. If two sets of shears were used, they could be installed a few feet apart so that one set would be certain to miss the connector and successfully cut through the drill pipe. Transocean had purchased and owned the blowout preventer, but BP had earlier specified a preventer with a single set of drill pipe shears.[14]

2. *Selection of the production riser*: As described earlier, a production riser is used to convey the pressurized oil and natural gas from the pay zone to the wellhead. It can be built in two forms: the "long string" that consists of an 8" diameter tube that extends all the way from the wellhead to the pay zone, or a "multi-string" that is built in sections that decrease in diameter as they descend and fit fairly snugly within the sections of the outer well casings that also decrease in diameter as they descend. The long-string form is much less expensive to purchase and to install. The multi-string form is much easier to cement in place because there is a much narrower opening between the outside of the

production riser and the inside of the well casing, thus forming a more secure plug in that annular route for escaping oil and natural gas. BP chose the long-string form.[15]

3. *Number of spacers for the production riser*: The long-string production riser that had been selected required special "spacers" for installation. Spacers were simple devices that could be attached at intervals to the riser pipe as that pipe was lowered into the surrounding well casing and keep that riser stably centered within the casing. Each spacer had three spring-loaded arms that ended in curved nylon (low friction) pads that pressed against the casing without causing damage. They were needed because, despite the sophisticated anti-roll and anti-pitch systems mounted on the supporting pontoons of the drilling platform, there was movement of that platform due to wave and wind forces, and that movement was first exaggerated by the height of the drilling derrick and then transmitted down the wire cable supporting the riser string before that string was finally cemented in place. The full length of the long-string model of riser had to be lowered to the well bottom before the cementing could occur, unlike the multi-string model with decreasing diameters that could be cemented after each 1,000′ section was put in place. The full length of the long-string riser for the Macondo well was four miles long. An 8″ diameter steel riser of that length, supported by a wire cable held by a tall derrick mounted on a moving platform would be bound, despite the obvious inertia, to move also, and that movement during the cementing process had the potential to create what were called "channels" in the cement seal. Fourteen spacers were needed to control the swaying and prevent those channels, but the decision to use the long strong riser had been made too close to the closure date. When BP ordered those spacers, their supplier in Houston had only six in stock. More spacers could be made, but that would take time and seriously delay the well closure. BP decided to move ahead, install the long-string riser and form the bottom cement seal with the existing six.[16]

Evidently, one of the supervising engineers on board the Deepwater Horizon was disappointed with that decision; he sent the following semi-complainant email to company officials in Houston:

> But, who cares; it's done, end of story. [We] will probably be fine and we'll get a good cement job. I would rather have to squeeze [get by with what we have] than get stuck above the WH [wellhead]."[17]

4. *Formula specifications for the sealing cement*: As was explained previously, the cement used in deepwater drilling has to be specially formulated to conform to the temperature, pressure, geological, and chemical conditions found at the site in order to be first pumped and then formed in place properly. At the Macondo well, it had been found that the pay zone rock strata fractured more easily than was common in most deepwater drilling sites, leading to what was termed "return loss" (escape of hydrocarbon fluids from the pay zone). To avoid that fracture, and that loss, it was desired to have a cement slurry that was highly fluid, and thus would flow more easily than normal, requiring less pressure that usual, back along the space between the outside of the riser pipe and the inside of the well bore within the pay zone up to the point where the riser pipe entered the protective casing, and then up the inside of that protective casing for a distance of 500'.

The cement fluidity could be increased by adding nitrogen gas during the mixing process. The desired result would be tiny bubbles throughout the mixture. The possible problem was that those tiny bubbles could coalesce during pumping, and create large bubbles or voids in the final seal. Halliburton, the cement contractor for the Macondo well, recommended against the use of nitrogen because of this danger, but apparently they never went ahead with needed laboratory tests under the temperature, pressure, and chemical conditions found at the Macondo site to support that recommendation. BP ordered a cement mixture with the nitrogen additive for the critical bottom cement seals.[18]

5. *Approval of test results for the bottom cement seals*: As was described earlier, the first or positive pressure test was quickly judged to have been successful. The pressure on the drilling mud within the well casing had been substantially increased, above the drill limit where it could be expected that any mud leaking outward through the seal would readily overcome the counterpressure of the oil and gas reserves inside the pay zone, thus resulting in a decrease in the recorded pressure within the riser. Here, when the pumps were turned off, there was no pressure decrease, and thus the positive pressure test was declared to have been successful.

The second or negative pressure test was not nearly so satisfying. Here the pressure on the drilling mud within the well casing had been substantially reduced, below the drill limit, where it could be expected that any oil or gas leaking through the bottom seal would quickly overcome the counterpressure of the drilling mud, and force an increase in the recorded pressure. This time, when the pumps were turned off, the pressure did quickly build back up again, indicating that pressurized fluids from the pay zone were leaking inward, past the recently formed cement seal.

It seemed impossible that the two tests could be so directly contradictory, that fluids of approximately the same density with approximately the same pressure differentials could leak inward through the cement seal but not outward through that same seal. This discrepancy started active discussions among those present as to the cause. Unfortunately, there were far too many people present. The drilling shack where the tests were being conducted was crowded. It was after 6:00 in the evening, and the two shifts were changing (it is traditional in deepwater drilling that the 12-hour shifts that are needed to keep the expensive drilling platforms fully productive change at 6:00 in the morning and at 6:00 in the evening). In addition, there was a group of visiting executives from Houston, two from BP and two from Transocean, who had been brought into the drilling shack as part of their scheduled tour of the drilling rig just before it was to be disconnected from the Macondo wellhead and towed to its next drilling assignment. These executives were being escorted by two senior drillers from Transocean and one supervising engineer from BP.

The executives and their escorts listened to what was obviously a serious discussion on a complex issue, but then the three onboard escorts decided that they and the four visiting executives were constraining that discussions and should move on. They continued their guided tour of the drilling platform, and left the decision on the reasons for the discrepancy between the positive and negative pressure test results to the two drilling crews directly responsible for those results. The foreman of the night shift gave his explanation of the cause, described in an earlier section, and recommended a different testing site, on an input pipe at the wellhead. This did record a constant pressure reading, and so was declared a success, and it was decided that the drawdown of the drilling mud could begin in order to install the final or safety cement plug at the midpoint of the riser pipe.[19]

Soon afterward this decision was made, the members of the day shift left the drill shack, heading for a much delayed dinner, though later testimony before the National Commission on the BP Deepwater Horizon Oil Spill revealed that they had left with considerable doubt about this recommended course of action:

Wheeler [the first shift foreman, and one of those killed in the blowout, explosion, and fire] was convinced that something wasn't right, recalled Christopher Pleasant [a BP supervisory engineer]. Wheeler couldn't believe the explanation he was hearing. But, his shift was up.[20]

6. *Cancelation of professional testing of the bottom cement seal:* To ensure that this next-to-last and the most critical step in the closure process did not have unrecognized problems, BP had contracted with Schlumberger to fly a team of three engineers from their Houston office out to the Deepwater Horizon early on the morning of April 20 to perform a series of additional tests to confirm the soundness of the newly installed bottom cement plugs.

According to the BP team's plan, if the cementing went smoothly, as it had, they could skip Schlumberger's cement evaluation...The decision was to send the Schlumberger team home on the 11:00 a.m. helicopter, thus saving time and the $128,000 fee.[21]

Troublesome Questions Raised by Those Specific Choices

A series of six decisions were made both prior to and then during the closure of the Macondo well that apparently were at least partially instrumental in bringing about the destructive blowout, explosion, and fire. All of these decisions, also apparently, were made to save money and time—and here time truly could be looked at as money given the $1 million per day fee charged for the rental of the Deepwater Horizon drilling platform—rather than to increase the level of protection against a possible blowout. These "cost savings are more important than safety improvements" decisions are—in our view—good examples of the cooperative acceptance culture that was described earlier in this chapter and that apparently dominated interactions among the different individuals, groups, and organizations on board the Deepwater Horizon at this time. Here, let us move on to eight very specific questions about those apparent "cost savings are more important than safety considerations" decisions and actions that—again in our view—have to be answered to understand the basic causes of the very destructive blowout, explosion, and fire:

1. *Blowout preventer:* Why did the involved managers at BP, doubtless after consulting with others in similar positions at Transocean (the owner and operator of the Deepwater Horizon that would purchase,

operate, and rely upon the safety of this device) specify a blowout preventer with a known 0.0333 probability of cutoff failure?

2. *Long-string riser*: Why did the involved managers at BP, doubtless after consultation with others in similar positions at Halliburton (the specialty cement contractor for the Macondo well) select the long-string riser despite the acknowledged difficulties of forming the cement seals that were so essential for well closure protection?

3. *Spacers for the risers*: And, why did those same involved mangers at BP require that the Transocean crew go ahead with the installation of the long riser pipe despite the lack of over half the needed riser spacers needed to center that pipe and prevent swaying movements in order to eliminate the danger of forming channels in the bottom cement plugs?

4. *Cement formulation for seals*: Why did the involved engineers at BP, against the explicit objections of the cement specialists at Halliburton, insist upon the use of the nitrogen-infused cement mixture to form the crucial bottom cement seals even though it was known that nitrogen had the potential to coalesce into bubbles—and possibly form leaks—within those seals?

5. *Negative pressure tests*: Why did the Transocean night-shift crew charged with performing the negative pressure test of the bottom cement seals ignore the obvious pressure increases that indicated that something was leaking into the well bore through either the bottom cement seals, the casing cement seals, or the wellhead input valves? Why not stop, and find out which route was at fault?

6. *Lack of objections by the visiting executives*: Why did the BP and Transocean executives who were present in the drill shack during the discussion of the discrepancies between the positive (leaking outward) and negative (leaking inward) pressure tests not participate? They meekly left the meeting at the urging of their onboard guides.

7. *Lack of objections by the day-shift members*: Why did the day-shift foreman not aggressively express his decided opinion that something was wrong with the positive pressure test? Why did he not suggest, "Look, try the negative test again; maybe we (the day shift) got the wrong result." Instead, all the members of that shift left because their "their shift was up."

8. *Lack of confirmatory testing*: Lastly, why did the BP supervisory engineers on board the Deepwater Horizon on the day of the blowout decide to send the Schlumberger team of contractor specialists who had flown

out to conduct a series of technologically advanced tests on the sound-ness of the bottom cement seals back home, without conducting those tests?

Problems in Logically Addressing the Troublesome Questions

Members of the National Commission on the BP Deepwater Horizon Oil Spill concluded in their Report to the President that there was a single answer to all eight of those questions, and that answer—and the cause of the blowout in their view—was a failure of management. They looked upon "management" as the groups of senior executives at the corporate headquarters of the three companies listed below who, they claimed, had failed to establish the decision standards and analytical methods needed to adjust for the risks of deepwater drilling:

> The well blew out because a number of separate risk factors, oversights and outright mistakes combined to overwhelm the safeguards meant to prevent just such an event from happening. But most of the mis-takes and oversights at Macondo can be traced back to a single over-arching failure: the failure of management. Better management by BP, Halliburton and Transocean would almost certainly have prevented the blowout by improving the ability of individuals involved to identify the risks they faced, and to properly evaluate, communicate and address them. A blowout in deepwater was not a statistical inevitability.[22]

We certainly agree that there was no single event or error that totally destroyed the Deepwater Horizon and severely damaged both the envi-ronment and the economy of the Gulf of Mexico. Instead, there were a series of interconnected events and errors that combined to produce those awful results. But, we do not at all agree that the fault can be directly traced back to the small groups of senior executives, assisted by their func-tional and technical staff members, at the corporate headquarters of those three named companies, who together allegedly had failed to improve "the ability of individuals involved to identify the risks they faced, and to properly evaluate, communicate, and address them.

It is easy to identify risks when risks are viewed as personal dangers. Every individual on board the Deepwater Horizon throughout both the standard drilling operations and the special closure procedures doubt-less was fully aware of the possibility of an unexpected event or accident that could injure or even kill members of the crew, including themselves.

Oil-well drilling since its beginning has been inherently recognized as a hard, dirty, risky occupation, and employees working in that industry tend be fully aware of the chance factors. They've seen far too many others injured or killed.

But, to "properly evaluate, communicate and address" those chance factors, it is necessary to step back, and look at risks as the product of statistical probabilities times financial impacts, not as individual worries. This requires a totally different approach that is managerial (it affects other people), not personal (it affects only yourself).

Each managerial decision or action—those eight described in the list of troubling questions provide very good examples—has a range of potential outcomes. Each outcome has a statistical probability of occurrence and a financial value of impact. For standard, ongoing activities—those that have not changed greatly over the past five to ten years—both the statistical probability and the financial value of each of those outcomes within that full range can be either directly derived or closely approximated from readily available historical data sets.

The problem here—at the Macondo well site—was that those historical data sets were not directly relevant. Too much had changed. This was among the first of the deepwater wells to be drilled at an ocean depth of one mile and to a well depth of an additional four miles, which brought much greater pressures and far larger problems. It would be possible, of course, to take the historical data sets, divide those data sets into groups by their depth range, look for trends in petroleum fluid and natural gas leakage between those groups as the depth and pressure increased, adjust those trends for the type of equipment employed and the nature of the pipes and compounds used, and then project those trends to the five mile total depth of the Macondo well, after it was completed, and just prior to its closure.

But suppose the relationship between the total depth of an oil well and the statistical probability and financial impact of a hard-to-control blowout, explosion, and fire is not linear, or curvilinear, but discontinuous. Suppose at some point the expected depth/risk relationships of a deepwater oil well simply fall apart.

Let us provide just one example of a possible discontinuous change at the Macondo well site. The supervising BP engineers on board the Deepwater Horizon had requested the infusion of nitrogen into the cement mixture that was to be used to form the bottom closure seals just prior to the blowout, explosion, and fire that totally destroyed the Deepwater Horizon and severely damaged both the environment and the economy of the region. The rock strata in this pay zone was known to be more easily fractured than normal, and it was thought desirable to use a lower than normal pumping pressure to force the cement outside the riser pipe that extended deep within the pay zone and then back along the space between that riser pipe and the well bore for a distance of 500′ up to the point where the riser pipe entered the protective casing of the well in order not to fracture that rock strata. It was expected that the nitrogen gas would form tiny bubbles within the cement mixture and thus form a more fluid, more easily pumped slurry.

But, it was known that the natural gas within the pay zone, under the extreme pressures and low temperatures within that zone, had been transformed into a liquid. What was the probability that the physical characteristics of the nitrogen gas infused into the cement mixture would also be changed, and perhaps coat the sand and gravel particles within that cement slurry in a way that would prevent proper adhesion. No one knew. Halliburton, the cement contractor for the Macondo well site, had recommended against the infusion of nitrogen because they believed that the expected tiny bubbles could easily coalesce during pumping into much larger bubbles, and create voids and gaps in the final seal. They wanted to perform laboratory tests under the temperature, pressure, and chemical conditions that existed at the site, but that would take time, delay the closure, and cost money. Their recommendation was rejected.

The problem with applying the economically rational approach recommended by the members of the National Commission on the BP Deepwater Horizon Oil Spill to the decisions and actions taken during the drilling and closure of the Macondo well was that the valid historical data sets simply did not exist, and the projection of the historical data sets that were available ignored the possibility—perhaps even the certainty, given the massive increases in fluid pressure and substantial decreases in local temperature of a four mile deep well beneath a one mile deep ocean—of our previously mentioned discontinuous change.

Discontinuous change cannot be projected. It has to be imagined. There were people on board the Deepwater Horizon who were worried about the cumulative effect of the "hurry up and get the job done" decisions and actions that were being taken. And maybe worry is a form of imagination. But those worried people did not speak up, probably because the modern technologies, the proven methods, the backup systems, and the trained employees that were now employed at just a very few deepwater drilling sites within the Gulf had convinced most participants and observers alike that a highly destructive blowout, explosion, and fire simply could no longer happen, certainly not on the scale that did occur.

We wish to propose a totally different approach. We believe that the cause of the uncontrolled blowout at the Macondo well in the Gulf of Mexico was not a failure of managerial methodology. *It was a failure of managerial responsibility.*

Definition of Managerial Responsibility

"Managerial responsibility" is an exceedingly imprecise term. But that does not mean that this is not a valid concept. Had any of the knowledgeable and experienced individuals who were present—the Transocean drilling foremen, the BP supervising engineers, the BP and Transocean visiting executives, and the Halliburton and Schlumberger contracting specialists—forcefully and convincingly expressed their views on any or all of those eight troubling questions listed earlier in this chapter, it is easy to assume that the Macondo oil-well blowout, explosion, and fire almost certainly would not have happened.

None of those foremen, engineers, executives, or specialists did express their views in a decided fashion. Yes, there a few muttered objections of the "Why worry; it's over and done with" or "I didn't like the explanation I was hearing but my shift was over" type. But no one spoke up forcefully, convincingly, and managerially. Why did that not happen?

One reason is the predominance of the culture of cooperative acceptance that encompasses so many of the horizontal joint ventures (multiple firms working together on a shared project or program at the same time and often on the same site) and vertical value chains (multiple firms producing jointly a common product or service in sequential stages and at different sites). Both are exceedingly common today given the technological skill competences and the competitive cost efficiencies that are so needed in so many markets and processes today. Here let us repeat our earlier explanation of this "to get along go along" culture. People who are working together for the successful completion of a large and complex project, program, or product but are employed by different corporations and have different job skills, different knowledge bases, different experience levels, different risk perceptions, different performance measures, and different incentive systems will, almost inevitably, develop a common pattern of cooperation and acceptance with which they feel jointly comfortable.

Another and, in our view, more valid reason for the failure of trained and experienced persons to speak out is the blunt explanation that none of them knew how to make a forceful and convincing presentation based upon personal concerns, not upon statistical probabilities and financial impacts. Acceptance of this argument will lead directly to a suitable two-stage definition of the currently imprecise construct of managerial responsibility:

> Managers are people in for-profit, non-profit, or governmental organizations who make decisions and take actions that often impact, in a mixture of both positive and negative ways, the well-being and rights of other individuals, groups, organizations, and even societies.
>
> Managerial responsibility, given the potential for both positive and negative impacts upon the well-being and rights of others, is the duty to logically think through the consequences and be prepared to fully explain the rationale of their proposed decisions and actions.

But, how does a manager logically think through and become fully prepared—but not personally obligated, a point we will defend later—to explain the rationale of his or her decisions or actions that may well impact, in a mixture of both positive and negative ways, the well-being and the rights of other individuals, groups, organizations, and even societies? This requires addressing the *nature* (to whom) and the *extent* (for what) of managerial responsibility, and applying the evaluative standards of economic efficiency, legal conformity, and personal integrity. These concepts and those constructs together form the basic theme and major contribution of this book, and will be briefly summarized in the form of an introduction to both in chapter 2.

CHAPTER 2

Proposing the Solution

What individuals, groups, organizations, and societies should people in managerial positions include in considering the *nature* of their managerial responsibilities? We assume that almost everyone will agree that managers have some degree of responsibilities to themselves, to their families, to the owners of the organizations at which they work, to the clients and customers served by those organizations, and to the other individuals and groups with whom they work within those organizations. Less clear, and doubtless more open to debate, are their responsibilities to the societies in which they live, and to the political and physical aspects of those societies.

It is difficult to envisage this very broad range of duties to very different individuals, groups, organizations, and societies. It is our suggestion that you look at the most basic elements within that range—yourself, your employer, and your society—as points in a triangular pattern, with graduations between those points (see figure 2.1). That is, you probably recognize responsibilities to yourself, and your family is the closest group between you and your society. Or, again, your workplace associates form the first and most familiar step between you and your employer.

Managers are bound to differ on how they would position themselves within this triangle that depicts their felt responsibilities toward others. Some might believe that it is a competitive world, and they should primarily look out for themselves and for their families. Others feel a substantial loyalty to their employers, and to their close associates at work. Still others are dedicated to their society, particularly if the term "society" is expanded to include the physical, political, and cultural as well as the social environments in which we live and work. We assume once again that we can all

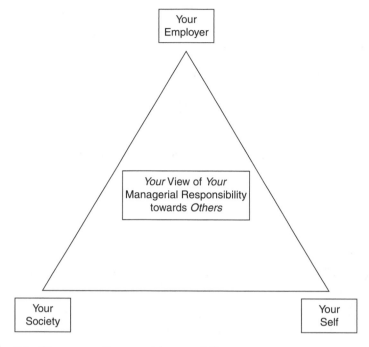

Figure 2.1   The nature of managerial responsibility.

agree that there is no "correct" position that everyone must take; instead, as was emphasized earlier, it is truly a matter of personal choice. And, we also assume we can all agree that at some point during the course of one's lifetime we should all begin to think logically and fully about that choice, about our pattern or balance of the responsibilities we feel to our selves, our employers, our societies, and the intervening individuals, groups, and organizations with whom we interact in various ways and at different times.

Now, how about the *extent* of those responsibilities to other people? Do managers also have responsibilities for outcomes? Again, we believe that we can all agree that clearly they do. Managers are people who make decisions and take actions, and these decisions and actions impact our selves, our employers, and our societies. Yet here also there are broad ranges of outcomes that are possible. What exactly does a manager owe to his or her employer in terms of outcomes? Increasing profits, expanding sales, improving products, bettering services, lowering costs, et cetera are all possible candidates. Perhaps once again it is necessary to get down to absolute basics, and for the employer the most essential duty might be economic efficiency: always produce the greatest output of wanted goods and services for the least input of limited resources. What does a manager owe to his or her society? Again there is a broad range of possible outcomes, but here the essential characteristic might be legal conformity: no special exemptions, always obey the law as written and adjudicated. Now the hardest issue of all, what does a manager own to himself or herself? Here the fundamental requirement might be personal integrity. *A literal translation of integrity is "wholeness": be a complete person, true to yourself, acting according your standards of conduct.*

Now, we come to the last of our "let us assume" arguments. Let us finally assume that you agree that people in managerial positions should decide for themselves upon a *rational balance* of the various "to whom" responsibilities they feel they owe to their employers, to their societies, and to themselves; that is, the *nature* of their personally felt responsibilities. Let us further assume that you also agree that those people in managerial positions should decide for themselves upon a *rational balance* of the "for what" responsibilities owed to those individuals, groups, organizations, and societies combining economic efficiency, legal conformity, and personal integrity; that is, the *extent* or range of those personally felt responsibilities (see figure 2.2).

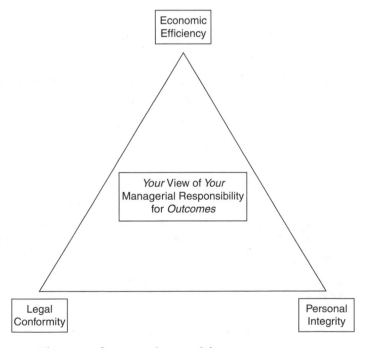

Figure 2.2 The extent of managerial responsibility.

The question then becomes the important one of how should managers attempt to achieve these personal and rational balances? That is, how should they logically think through the decisions and actions they believe that their organizations should take when faced with complex and awkward situations that truly do concern them, and—most important of all—*how do they logically convince others, those above, those equal, and those below them within their organizational structure as well as those outside that organizational structure who have the abilities and the resources to influence the potential outcomes to join in the effort and provide the support that is needed for the successful completion of a given plan, policy, or program?*

That last is a long sentence but an important one. The recommendation of this book is that managers should start by (a) recognizing that individuals differ in their standards of conduct that are based upon their personal goals, norms, beliefs, and values; and by (b) understanding that situations differ in their impacts upon individuals, groups, organizations, and societies. A decision or action that one person might believe to be fully appropriate might strike another as totally wrong. It is necessary for managers to deal with these conflicts in a logically convincing manner, and our version of that manner is shown in figure 2.3, with an explanation of each of the seven steps commencing below.

Understand the Different Standards

Most people, when they first encounter a situation in which the well-being of some individuals, groups, organizations, or societies are going to be hurt or harmed in some way, or in which the rights of those or other individuals, groups, organizations, or societies are going to be compromised

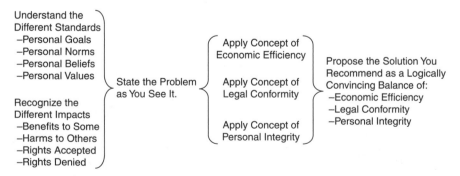

Figure 2.3 Steps in the analytical process for the determination of managerial responsibility.

or ignored in some other way, turn first to their personal standards of personal conduct. These personal standards are frequently termed "moral," but that latter term has an exceedingly wide range of normative—"you must always act this way"—interpretations. We much prefer the term "personal"—"you decide how you should act"—and thus each person's chosen set of standards becomes that individual's intuitive gauge both of his or her own behavior and that of the other individuals, groups, organizations, and societies with whom he or she interacts. These individually selected standards thus form the means all of us first turn to in deciding whether our decisions and actions, and those of the other people, groups, organizations, and even societies with whom we live, work, and associate, are in our view "right" or "wrong," "just" or "unjust," "fair" or "unfair."

The problem—and the reason for the quotation marks, often termed "sneer marks" by concerned moral philosophers—is that there are no precisely worded and widely accepted definitions of those six terms. What exactly, for example, does "fair" mean? We much prefer the term "legitimate," which can be defined as "conforming to recognized principles or accepted rules or standards"[1] and will use that word throughout this book. We will also do our best to supply enough "recognized principles or accepted rules or standards" so that—though they may not be fully recognized, widely accepted, or universally applied—they do combine to provide *logically convincing support* for managerial decisions or actions that impact the well-being and the rights of other individuals, groups, organizations, and societies in ways that may well turn out to be positive for some, negative for others, and a mixture for everyone else.

We realize that this search for what is legitimate (meaning "supported" in the pages of most dictionaries) rather than for what is right or just or fair (meaning "good" in the minds of most individuals, but without any widely understood demarcation between what is thought to be "good" versus what is thought to be "bad") will seem to be a retreat from a critical issue to many if not most readers. But, let us repeat once again, our intention is to demonstrate how managers can be logically convincing in those situations where the outcome of a given decision or action may well turn out to be fully positive for some, highly negative for others, and a mixture of those two for everyone else. Let us provide just one example from the prior chapter to justify that preference.

A team of three engineers from Schlumberger had flown out to the Deepwater Horizon early on the morning of the approaching blowout, explosion, and fire to conduct a series of advanced technology tests on the integrity of the bottom cement seals that had been installed during the previous day as the next-to-last step in the closure of the Macondo well. The BP supervising engineers on that drilling platform who were overseeing the closure process decided to send that team back to their home office in Houston, without conducting the planned tests, to save $128,000 and avoid an additional day's delay in the closure process that, given the high rent for the use of the drilling platform and the high pay for the service of the drilling crew, would have added another $1,000,000 to the overhead costs. Both the service charge to Schlumberger and the overhead charge from Transocean would have had to been paid by BP.

This "keep 'em here" or "send 'em home" decision was not an easy one for the BP supervising engineers to make. There were performance implications for the engineers, profit consequences for their employer, and safety worries about their society. Saying that it was "right" to send the Schlumberger testing crew back to their home office would not have added anything to the understanding or conviction of the others involved. Someone else would just have responded that such an action was "wrong," and then there would be a heated argument rather than a rational discussion.

Instead, our recommendation is that the BP supervisor engineers should have looked for support from: (a) the evaluative constructs of economic efficiency ("Does this make the best use of our least wanted resources to produce our most wanted goods and services, while including all potential external costs?"); (b) legal conformity ("Does this adhere to the law as written and as adjudicated, or is this possible only because of gaps, omissions, or obsolete portions of that law?"); and (c) personal integrity (You will find that "Can we be open, honest, truthful, and proud of what we plan to do?" is one of seven suggested measures of personal integrity). This would not have taken as much time nor have been as complex as the supervising engineers from BP and the operating mangers from Transocean (had they been included in the decision) might initially have expected.

There certainly was concern among some if not many of the experienced persons in managerial positions on board the Deepwater Horizon that too many corners were being cut too closely. Had those concerned managers and engineers put together a logically convincing decision to conduct the advanced series of tests, and had they then found the defects that obviously must have existed within one or more of the bottom cement plugs, they would have preserved the lives of 11 of their coworkers, avoided the injuries to nearly 80 others, saved their employers untold billions of dollars in cleanup expenses and remedial fees, fines, and judgments, and saved the environment and the economy of the Gulf from long-lasting damage. They might even with luck—because preventing a catastrophic outcome almost never shows up on annual performance reviews with the frequency and force that causing such an outcome almost inevitably does—have received a decent bonus, or maybe even a promotion.

Instead, the BP supervising engineers made their decision relying solely upon the evaluative construct of economic efficiency. That reliance, as it turned out, was not fully rational for they left out the important element in the efficiency construct termed "external costs," which are any costs imposed upon others without their consent. These costs are frequently omitted when there is a lack of historical data—as there definitely was in this instance—that made it impossible to accurately estimate the statistical probabilities and the financial values of the range of potential outcomes that could come from a failure to discover that the bottom cement plugs had not been solidly formed in place. If one leaves out the external costs of managerial decisions and actions that obviously have the potential for harmful social, environmental, and/or financial impacts, then almost any of that type of infrequently encountered but obviously damaging managerial decision or action will have a positive mean expected value. We are attempting in this book to supply a rational alternative for the calculation of mean expected values under conditions of uncertainty, not risk.[2]

Our argument, and in our view, one of the more important messages of this book, is that it is necessary to look at both the costs imposed upon others without their consent and the rights denied to others, also without their consent, from multiple lenses. The reason for these different lenses is not to be able to compute a financial equivalent for the reduction in well-being or the limitation on rights through other means—for that is obviously impossible given the lack of relevant historical data—but to look at those reductions in well-being and limitations of rights from the combined logical perspectives of economic efficiency, legal conformity, and personal integrity. Those three constructs when used jointly tend to adjust for the imperfections that are found within each individually.

Before moving on to a description of those three evaluative constructs, let us look at the sources of each individuals personal standards of conduct, the means by which most people judge what they believe to be right and just and fair, rather than what—in our preferred approach—they could accept as being legitimate.

Figure 2.4 Causes of variations in the personal standards of conduct.

Personal standards of conduct differ between individuals because the goals, norms, beliefs, and values upon which they depend also differ, and those goals, norms, beliefs, and values in turn differ because of variations in the religious and cultural traditions and the economic and social situations in which the individuals are immersed. These relationships are shown in figure 2.4, and the terms are defined in the following text.

1. *Personal goals*: Goals are preferred outcomes. They are the things we want out of life and the things we expect others probably want out of life as well. They include material possessions (money, homes, cars, and boats), lifestyle preferences (power, position, influence, and health), personal relationships (family, friends, associates, and respect), and social aims (justice, equality, a clean environment, and a world at peace). If one person wants more money and power and another wants greater justice and equality, then probably they are going to differ on what they consider to be legitimate (once again, "conforming to recognized principles or accepted rules or standards) on many major issues.

   Doubtless most individuals when considering their personal standards of conduct will continue to use the far more familiar terms of "right versus wrong," "fair versus unfair," or "just versus unjust," but as we have explained previously, we much prefer the contrast of "legitimate versus non-legitimate" because that contrast leads more naturally to group discussions about the insight provided by reasoning from a variety of principles, rules, and standards rather than to interpersonal arguments about the primacy of any single principle, rule, or standard.

2. *Personal norms*: Norms are preferred behaviors. They are the ways we expect to act and the ways in which we expect others to act in given situations. Personal norms differ from personal standards in that the norms have no close association with judgments about what a given individual believes to be "right or wrong" or—in our terms— "legitimate or non-legitimate." Personal norms are expectations of behavior; personal standards are evaluations of behavior. People in the United States expect you to drive on the right-hand side of the road; that is a norm. If you persist in driving on the left-hand side (in the United States and most of Western Europe, though not in the United Kingdom), then they will say that you are "wrong"; that is a standard based upon conformity with the law.

3. *Personal beliefs*: Beliefs are preferred thoughts. They are the ways we expect to think, and the ways in which we expect others to think, about given situations. Our beliefs generally support our norms, and our norms usually lead toward our goals. For example, the two coauthors of this book believe that cigarette smoke causes cancer, and consequently we expect you not to smoke in our presence because one of our shared goals is good health. If you persist in smoking, despite our repeated (and perhaps even heated) objections, we are going to say that you are "wrong"—even we will not then use the far weaker sounding term "non-legitimate" in this particular situation—for you have acted against our personal standard of conduct derived from our goals, norms, and beliefs.

4. *Personal values*: Values are our priorities between goals, norms, and beliefs. They are the ways we judge the relative importance of what we want to achieve, how we expect to act, and why we believe as we do. Most people do not consider that all of their goals, norms, and beliefs are of equal importance. Generally, there are some that seem more important, more "valued" than others. Here let us use an example not limited to traffic rule compliance or smoking objection adjustment, but far greater in application and much higher in importance. We assume that most residents of the free world generally support equal voting rights for all citizens (the advantages of participatory democracy constitute a "belief" among both those who now enjoy that form of government and those who wish they had it). If agents

for a political party within a given country of their residency offered each citizen a sum of money (increases in well-being, even though small, constitute a "goal" for many if not most individuals) to vote a certain way (counter to the "norm" of many if not most citizens), we assume that offer would be angrily rejected by a large majority of those citizens, with the accusation that such an offer was "wrong." Why? We would venture to say that a large percentage of the population valued their belief in participatory democracy and their norm of voter independence far more than they did their goal of smallish increases in financial well-being.

5. *Cultural and religious traditions*: The goals, norms, beliefs, and values of a person frequently vary depending upon the cultural and religious traditions of that person, and those variations will in turn affect his or her personal standards of conduct. Managerial personnel at all levels, functions, and competences are becoming increasingly diverse in their cultural and religious traditions. Clearly, it is important not to stereotype those differences, but it is necessary to recognize their possible impacts upon the goals, norms, beliefs, and values of different individuals, and consequently upon their personal standards of conduct.

6. *Economic and social situations*: The goals, norms, beliefs, and values of a person will also vary depending upon the economic and social situation of that person. The economic situation includes the relative income and financial security of the individual. The social situation does not refer to the relative status or standing of a given person within a particular society; instead, it considers that person's membership in various groups and organizations whose goals, policies, and programs tend to influence each members individual goals, norms, beliefs, values and—ultimately—his or her personal standards of conduct. Clearly once again, it is necessary not to stereotype these economic and social differences, but it is necessary to consider their possible influence upon intuitive judgments of what they believe to be "right versus wrong," and what we—hopefully for the last time, at least within this chapter—consider to be "legitimate versus non-legitimate."

Recognize the Different Impacts

Managerial responsibility problems have earlier been described as being complex because they result in benefits for some and cause harms to others, and because they recognize the rights of some and ignore the rights of others. That combination of benefits and harms, and that mixture of rights acknowledged and rights ignored, together compose the "impacts" of a given decision or action. Those impacts—the benefits and harms, the rights accepted and rights denied—are what people think about when they consider a proposed decision or action with which they feel uncomfortable because it appears to go against one or more of their personal standards of conduct.

A good example here might be the decision of the foreman of the second-shift drilling crew who had declared the negative pressure test of the bottom cement seals to have been successful despite the continued rise in pressure at the customary recording site for that test. A normal first thought of the other individuals associated in some way with that decision and the following action might well have been, "Who is likely to get hurt if the bottom well seals do fail just as we start drawing down the drilling mud and thus reducing the counterpressure in order to put in the last-step safety cement plug halfway up the riser?"

As was described in the first chapter of this book, most of the people working on board the Deepwater Horizon must have been fully aware of the dangers of offshore drilling—the 1,550 injuries, 60 deaths, and 948 fires and explosions that had occurred in the Gulf of Mexico from 2001 to 2010—and that awareness probably influenced their own personal standards of conduct. Why, once again, did no one object? A normal second thought of those associated individuals who felt that the decision was improper might well have been, "If I raise objections the foreman and those supervising engineers together are going to tell me that everybody on board this rig—including me—will benefit from getting this conversion to production job done quickly, without further delay or greater cost, and I wouldn't know how to make my case against that conclusion." Our suggested rule is that if you want to "make your case" get *all* of the impacts out, both positive and negative, right at the start:

1. *Benefits*: Whose well-being will be substantially improved by the current or proposed decision or action of a person in a managerial position? Focus on material or financial or lifestyle benefits to directly involved individuals, groups, organizations, or societies, not to distant corporations, communities, or countries for whom little sympathy normally is felt. Managerial responsibility problems involve a mixture of well-being outcomes, both positive and negative. First, list the positive ones, the benefits. Specifically, identify the major individuals,

groups, organizations, or societies whose well-being you believe will be improved, and give a short description of the nature of those improvements.

2. *Harms*: Whose well-being will be substantially reduced by the current or proposed decision or action by a person in a managerial position? Focus here also on material or financial or lifestyle harms to directly involved individuals, groups, organizations, or societies, not to distant corporations, communities, or countries. Managerial responsibility problems, once again, constitute a mixture of well-being outcomes, both positive and negative. Now, list the negative ones. Identify the major individuals, groups, organizations, or societies whose well-being you believe will be reduced, and give once again a short description of the nature of that reduction.

3. *Rights accepted*: Whose rights will be exercised and made more certain by the present or proposed decision or action of a person in a managerial position? This is an important issue that should be addressed because many people in managerial positions feel that they not only have a right but a duty to decide and act in certain ways. Focus on the recognition of rights for all involved individuals, groups, organizations, or societies, not on those of distant companies, communities, or countries. Be selective. Make certain that there is a clear recognition of a legitimate right to do something where that recognition will positively affect the way in which those individuals, groups, organizations are able to pursue their goals. Identify the individuals, groups, organizations, or societies whose rights you believe will be recognized or expanded in some important way, and give an adequate description of the nature of those rights.

4. *Rights denied*: Whose rights will be ignored and made less certain by the present or proposed action of a person in a managerial position? This is one of the most important issues that must be included because many people react strongly when they feel that their rights are "on the line" and are in danger of being either ignored, reduced, or taken away. Focus on the infringements of rights for all involved individuals, groups, organizations, or societies, not on those of distant companies, communities, or countries. Again, be selective. Make certain that there is a clear infringement of a legitimate right to do something where that infringement will negatively affect the way those individuals, groups, organizations, or societies are able to pursue their goals. Identify the

individuals, groups, organizations, or societies whose rights you believe will be ignored or lessened in some important way, and give an adequate description of the nature of those rights.

State the Problem as You See It

If your listed balance of benefits received and harms imposed, and your described contrast of rights accepted and rights denied, conflict with your personal standards of conduct, then *you* face what we would term a problem in the nature and the extent of *your* managerial responsibility.

We want to emphasize once again, however, that in our view no one—including the authors of this book—has such dominant knowledge of both human character and social conduct that they can tell you authoritatively to *whom* you are responsible, for *what* you are responsible, and consequently *how* you should act. You have to work all that out for yourself. Your only responsibility, in our view once again, is: (a) to identify in your own mind the balance of impacts—both positive and negative—upon the well-being and rights of other individuals, groups, and organizations who will be affected by the currently proposed managerial decision or action; (b) to conceive in your own mind an alternative decision or action that you believe will have a more legitimate (conforming to recognized principles or accepted rules or standards) balance of those impacts upon those others; and (c) to prepare in your own mind the reasons you believe that those acknowledged principles, rules, or standards will logically support the alternative decision or action that you may wish to propose.

In short, you are free to take a stand, or not to take a stand, as you see fit. But, remember that—due to the differences in personal standards of conduct that come from variations in the goals, norms, beliefs, and values of others, and from the differences in the religious and cultural traditions and the economic and social situations in which those others find themselves—if you do indeed take a stand, others may not agree with you.

To convince others, if you do decide to take a stand and speak out firmly, you will at the start want to get everyone else involved in the situation to fully comprehend your point of view. Your first few sentences, in either a verbal conversation or a written report, are the critical ones. You want the individuals to whom you are speaking or writing to begin thinking, "You know, maybe this guy (either man or woman in modern parlance) does have a valid point."

Start with a non-accusatory statement expressing your concerns about a proposed decision or action or an existing situation, with a brief summary of the facts supporting those concerns. Then suggest the two most obvious alternatives, usually either to stay with the current decision, action, or situation or to make a major change in that decision, action or situation. List the possible outcomes, stressing the uncertainty, and the potential impacts of those outcomes. Give your recommendation as to what should be done, why you believe this should be done, *and stop*. Give others a chance to respond.

The following is our recommendation for a statement of the problem that might well have been effective had it been raised in the crowded drill shack as the members of the second shift prepared to declare the negative pressure test of the bottom cement seals a success while four members of the first shift, four visiting executives from BP and Transocean, and two supervisory engineers from BP listened:

> You know, I'm worried about the way we (always use the collective "we"; otherwise you assign blame and encourage opposition) are making this decision about the meaning of the negative pressure test. The positive pressure test was fine; it showed that there were no fluids—that is, drilling mud—leaking out of the well bore into the pay zone. But this negative pressure test seems to show that there were some fluids leaking into the well bore, maybe drilling mud from the well head, but much worse if those liquids were petroleum-based compounds coming from that big pay zone we've struck.
>
> We have two choices. We can go ahead, declare the negative pressure test a success, and start to pump out the drilling mud, replace that mud with sea water and begin to form the safety cement plug halfway up the riser. That mud replacement process will lower the counterpressure within the well, and create a brief period of increased danger for a blowout. Maybe nothing is going to happen. We may well be fine, finish on time, and save a bucket of money for the owners and operators of our platform.
>
> But, if there truly is an inward leak in one of those bottom cement plugs, things can get awfully ugly awfully fast given the very high pressures that exist down there. There could be major injuries to the crew, severe damages to the rig, and large expenses to the owners and operators as we all try to shut down the flow from the highly pressurized, easily fractured, and exceedingly large oil and gas reserve we're tapped into.

Instead of going ahead with this last but potentially dangerous "draw down pressure to form the final safety plug" step in the closure, my recommendation is that we stop, go back, and try to find the source of the fluids leaking into the well bore. That will take time and cost money. And, there is no way to compare the costs and benefits of doing that rather than continuing as is because we don't know what's going to happen if we continue as is. No one has ever encountered this situation under *deepwater* (emphasize this) conditions before. There is no law that says we must go back and try to find the causes for the discrepancies in the test results because we have one solidly successful and one explainably successful test result, and according to the law that's all we need.

But, I've always followed one very basic rule in my working life: to always be open, honest, truthful, and *proud* of what I do. That's why I'm being open and honest now, and why I want to be proud in the future about the decision that I hope we all will make—expensive in both time and money though it may be—to go back and find the sources of the negative "inward" leak, and thus be certain that what we're doing will turn out to be the best for everybody in the long run.

This may seem such an obvious and simple argument to make, with just a short listing of benefits and harms, no mention of rights, and only brief allusions to economic efficiency, legal conformity, and personal integrity. But, it should be remembered that no one in fact did make that argument—however simple it might seem—while present at that meeting. And, it should also be remembered that here was a situation in which similar errors and mistakes had built up on this site over time, doubtless recognized by many of those present in the drill shack, to create what—after it did happen—can only be described as a physical, financial, and personal disaster of the greatest proportion for all of the individuals, groups, and organizations involved with the Deepwater Horizon, for the population directly on shore, and for the environment and the economy of the full Gulf region.

Let us say that you were indeed one of the supervising engineers or operating managers who had been on board the Deepwater Horizon through much of the drilling and was now on board during the closing of that well. Let us also say that the series of shortcuts and cost savings that had occurred during the drilling and continuing into the closing did conflict with your personal standards of personal conduct. Let us lastly say that you had, at some point in your past, heard about and accepted a definition of managerial responsibility as the duty for persons in managerial positions to logically think through all of their decisions or actions that have the potential to harm the well-being and damage the rights of other individuals, groups, organizations, and societies. Given those three conditions then we believe that you would find that increased fluency in economic efficiency, legal conformity, and personal integrity, together with an understanding of the problems that afflict each of those forms of reasoning, would be useful in order to be convincing. This chapter ends with a brief summary of the positive and negative aspects of those three constructs. Our comments here will indeed be just summaries. Fuller explanations of the theories and—particularly—the citations to their sources will be provided in the three chapters that follow this one.

Apply the Evalative Construct of Economic Efficiency

"Economic efficiency" refers to the belief that the major function of all organizations, whether for-profit, non-profit, or governmental in nature, is to either produce or facilitate the production of the greatest volume of the most-wanted goods and services at the smallest usage of the least wanted financial, material, and individual resources. Given that those most-wanted goods and services are sold through competitive output markets and that those least wanted resources are purchased though competitive input markets, then the benefits extend: (a) to the customers and clients of all of those productive organizations through impartially determined prices for their purchased goods and services; and (b) to the suppliers of all of those productive organizations through impartially determined prices for their offered monies, materials, and skills.

Customers for the goods and services and suppliers of the monies, materials, and skills combine to constitute nearly everyone within society (except for the unemployed, and it is generally assumed that they will be brought more fully into this buy-and-supply society through public assistance programs). Therefore maximum efficiency among for-profit, non-profit, and governmental organizations can be said to result in maximum benefits for the full society.

Economic efficiency, therefore, meets our requirements to be used as one of the theoretical constructs for evaluating the decisions and actions of managers that often impact, in both positive and negative ways, the well-being and rights of others because it includes all individuals, all organizations, and all societies. In short, it can be said to be universal (applicable to everyone), absolute (with exceptions for no one), impartial (without favoritism for any one), and basic (understandable by all).

There are, however, some problems with this universal, absolute, impartial, and basic evaluative construct of economic efficiency. The problems are the assumptions that: (a) all input and output markets are fully competitive; (b) all input suppliers and all output customers are fully informed; and (c) all external costs are fully recognized and included in the purchase prices. Chapter 3 will more fully describe this relationship theory of economic efficiency, and the problems imposed by the all too frequent neglect of these three essential assumptions.

For now, we would just like to ask you to accept that economic efficiency is a totally rational theory of the exchange relationships between suppliers, producers, and customers that, due to the impartiality of markets, benefit all within society. We are now going to briefly apply this rational theory—or "evaluative construct" in our terms—to the managerial decisions and actions that apparently combined to increase the probability of the highly destructive blowout, explosion, and fire on board Deepwater Horizon drilling platform at the Macondo well site in the Gulf of Mexico. There were eight of these decisions or actions described in chapter 1.

1. *Blowout preventer*: The involved managers at BP (the owner of the Macondo well site), doubtless after consulting with others in similar positions at Transocean (the owner and operator of the Deepwater Horizon), decided to purchase a blowout preventer with a known 3.33 out of 100 probability of cutoff failure.

2. *Long-string riser*: The involved managers at BP, doubtless after consultation with others in similar positions at Halliburton (the specialty cement contractor for the Macondo well site), selected the long-string riser pipes despite the acknowledged difficulties of forming the bottom cement seals that were so essential for well closure protection.

3. *Spacers for the riser*: The involved mangers at BP insisted that the Transocean crew go ahead with the installation of the long-string riser pipe despite the lack of over half the riser spacers that were needed to center the riser and prevent swaying movements so that there would be less danger of forming gaps or channels in the bottom cement seals.

4. *Cement formulation for seals*: The involved engineers at BP, against the explicit objections of the cement specialists at Halliburton, insisted upon the use of the nitrogen-infused cement mixture to form the

crucial bottom cement seals even though nitrogen had the potential to coalesce into bubbles—and possibly form leaks—within those seals.

5. *Negative pressure tests*: The Transocean night-shift crew charged with performing the negative pressure test on the bottom cement seals essentially ignored the obvious pressure increases that indicated that something was leaking into the well bore through the bottom cement seals, the casing cement seals or the wellhead input valves.

6. *Lack of objections by the visiting executives*: The BP and Transocean executives who were present in the drill shack during the discussion of the discrepancies between the positive (leaking outward) and negative (leaking inward) pressure tests did not enter into the discussion. They meekly left the meeting at the urging of their onboard guides.

7. *Lack of objections by the day-shift members*: The Transocean day-shift foreman did not express his decided opinion that something was wrong with the positive pressure test. Instead, he and other members of the day-shift crew meekly left the meeting because "their shift was up."

8. *Lack of confirmatory testing*: The BP supervisory engineers on board the Deepwater Horizon on the day of the blowout decided to send the Schlumberger team of contractor specialists who had flown out to conduct a series of technologically advanced tests on the soundness of the bottom cement seals back home, without conducting those tests.

In all of these decisions and actions, it is clear that the markets were competitive (prices were negotiated in most of the exchanges) and that the participants were informed (almost all were petroleum engineers or geological scientists), but that the external costs were never considered. Thus they were not added to the costs of the purchased machines, pipes, compounds, and services as required in the most dominant theory of managerial practice: economic efficiency.

Why did this happen? The answer is very simple. There were no historical data points to establish the full range of possible outcomes—both positive and negative—for any of those decisions or actions, or to compute the statistical probability and the financial value of each of the differing outcomes within that range. This was the first of the deepwater wells to reach a five mile depth using a specially designed and remarkably stable drilling platform, staffed by a specially trained crew and equipped with automated controls and redundant safety mechanisms. As explained in chapter 1, there was a general feeling on board the Deepwater Horizon that, while leaks and accidents were bound to occur as a natural consequence of oil well drilling, a highly destructive blowout, explosion, and fire simply could no longer occur. Consequently, the persons in managerial positions who made those decisions or took those actions totally forgot about the external costs.

We need something else to ensure the consideration of the frequently forgotten assumptions that underlie the optimal social benefits at minimal social costs theory of economic efficiency. Those assumptions, let us repeat one last time, are that all input resource and output product markets are fully competitive, all input suppliers and output customers are fully informed, and all external costs are fully included.

Maybe this "something else" that is needed is legal conformity. Certainly it should be possible, within a democratic society to establish the rules and set the standards for fully competitive input and output markets, fully informed suppliers and customers, and fully included external costs. The next section summarizes the evaluative construct of legal conformity.

Obviously, it was not possible for either legislative bodies or regulatory agencies to do a better job of forecasting the statistical probabilities and financial values of future outcomes than the managers on site, given their similar lack of historical data. But could they not have set more stringent standards for blowout preventers, riser pipes, riser spacers, cement formulations, and pressure tests based upon the historical data from shallow-depth and medium-depth wells adjusted for deepwater conditions within the Gulf of Mexico? Did those standards exist, and was the problem here that the managers and engineers who had ignored the external costs also refused to conform to the existing laws? Here we come to the evaluative construct of legal conformity.

Apply the Evaluative Construct of Legal Confomity

In an ideal world, all that a person in a managerial position would need to do to decide what actions he or she should either take, or recommend be taken, when faced with a perceived problem in which some individuals, groups, or organizations were going to be benefited while others could be harmed, or in which some of those same individuals, groups, or organization were going to have their rights recognized while others could see their rights rejected, would be to apply the twin evaluative constructs of economic efficiency and legal conformity.

But, we don't live in an ideal world. We live in a highly contentious and rapidly changing global environment in which the assumptions underlying the evaluative construct of economic efficiency are often forgotten and those underlying the evaluative construct of legal conformity are often ignored. Chapter 4 will describe, in some detail, the content of the law, the formation of the law, the practice of the law, the claimed impartiality of that practice, and the assumptions underlying that claimed impartiality. Here, we just briefly wish to summarize each of those areas:

1. *Content of the law*: Law can be viewed as set of rules that prescribe the ways in which individuals, groups, and organizations within a given society should act in their relationships with other individuals, groups, or organizations throughout that same society under similar conditions. But, it is difficult to define those actions, those relationships, and those conditions with adequate precision. Think for a moment about how you would write a requirement for the inclusion of "it's never-happened-before" external costs for the deepwater drilling sector of the petroleum industry.

2. *Formation of the law*: It is also possible to view the law as the natural outgrowth of the personal standards of conduct held by a majority of the members of a given democratic society. This outgrowth is a slow, laborious, and frequently conflict-ridden process. As a result, many of our laws are not as uniform in their definitions, as universal in their applications, as focused in their intentions, or as current in their solutions as many of us would like them to be.

3. *Practice of the law*: The frequently imprecise content of law, the often divisive formation of law, and the intensifying competition of the global economy have jointly brought about a major change in the practice of law. Law firms are now frequently requested by their clients to find gaps, omissions, and non-current portions of existing laws that will permit profitable actions but may have the potential to harm others. Law firms pledge to "zealously defend" their clients' rights to take those actions before impartial judges and juries.

4. *Definition of justice in law*: Disputes frequently arise over the use of these gaps, omissions, and non-current portions of the law that are beneficial to one party but may be harmful to others. It is now claimed that when both parties employ competent law firms to argue the facts of the case and the law of the land before impartial judges and juries in open courtrooms, the result is essentially "competitive justice."

5. *Problems with competitive justice in law*: Instead of competitive markets, we now have competitive attorneys. The argument is that the defects in

the formation of law no longer matter because laws are now more adjudicated before impartial judges than enacted by non-impartial legislators. The underlying assumptions are that all contending parties have equal financial resources to retain equally competent law firms. Money and contacts are needed by the contending parties and experience and size are essential for the law firms.

We fear that we may have appeared to be overly condemning of legislative members and practicing attorneys in this short summary. Chapter 4 on legal conformity is, of course, much longer and, in our view, comes across as more balanced. Here let us conclude by saying that many reputable legal practitioners and respected legal scholars essentially make the argument that this "zealous representation of contending parties before impartial deciders over the interpretation of imperfect laws" is as close as it is possible to get to the goal of justice. Before we settle for this particular "as close as we can get" alternative, it might be well to consider what we really mean when we use the term "justice." In short, it might be well to attempt to define justice. This is an area of study that seems to lie halfway between the philosophy of law and the philosophy of life, and so let us move on to the next evaluative construct, that of personal integrity, the portion of human character that essentially can be said to represent an individual's philosophy of life.

Apply the Evaluative Construct of Personal Integrity

It is necessary to start by accepting the fact that justice exists as an ideal rather than as a reality. It remains an ideal because—unfortunately—we live in a world of imperfect human beings who divide their personal goals between those of self-interest, organizational interest, and social interest in varying degrees under varying conditions at varying times. It is possible to think generally about different principles that would—if all of us would agree to follow the same universal (applicable to everyone), absolute (with exceptions for no one), impartial (without favoritism for any one), and basic (understandable by all) standards or rules devised from such a principle—enable us to overcome some of our human imperfections and bring our ideal of justice closer to our reality of life. But, we can't really get all the way to a totally just world.

We can't really get all the way to a totally just world because individual human beings simply will not universally agree to absolutely follow any obviously impartial and easily understood principle, standard, or rule.

One of the imperfections of human character is the propensity almost all of us have to attempt to achieve our particular set of mixed self-interest, organizational-interest, and social-interest goals by ignoring, bypassing, or breaking any externally imposed and/or widely recommended principles, rules, or standards of conduct with which we disagree.

The result is that scholars have been unable—despite 25 centuries of trying—to define justice. Most people have simply given up on searching for an adequate definition of what truly is "just," and instead rely upon meaningless synonyms such as "equitable," "proper," or "fair." We believe that we have not given up when we use the term "legitimate" because legitimacy is based upon a series of principles, rules, and standards *designed to improve the impartiality of the process rather than to define the goal of the society.* We admit that we cannot define justice either, but—in our view—impartiality along multiple routes can bring us awfully close.

Why can't anyone define justice? We realize that we have partially covered this "difficulty of definition" topic earlier within this chapter during the discussion of personal standards of conduct, but here we are dealing with the much broader and more important goal of social standards of conduct so please bear with us. Our view is that there are three reasons:

1. *Human character*: There are the previously mentioned imperfections in human character that make it impossible to demonstrate that a given principle, standard, or rule would inevitably lead to the ideal outcome of justice. Some independent-minded individual, group, or organization within society will inevitably get off the bus, lead the revolt, or win the election.

2. *Interwoven concept*: Justice is too interwoven a concept with too important a set of societal, political, and economic consequences. Those consequences impact both the well-being and the rights of all individuals, groups, organizations within society, and well-being and rights are totally different constructs, diverse rather than parallel, and vitally important to all.

3. *Structured impartiality:* The causal factor of justice has to be structured impartiality. That structure can be found in the market forces of economic efficiency, the judges and juries of legal conformity, and the decision guides of personal integrity. But, all have underlying assumptions. Let us move on to examining the nature—and assumptions—of personal integrity.

"Personal integrity" refers to the *completeness or wholeness* of a person. The root words, of course, are "integer," which means a whole number, and "integral," which means a single unit of related parts. When we say that a given individual "has integrity," we mean that such a person comes complete with a consistent set of goals, norms, beliefs, and values that together form the conduct standards of that person, and that don't vary over time or bend with conditions. In short, integrity in a person means that what you see in his or her character is what you're going to get in his or her decisions and actions.

We want to emphasize, however, that personal integrity in our view goes far beyond the commonly prescribed behavioral norms of being honest, telling the truth, and keeping one's word. If the authors of this book, to provide a demeaning but we assure you fictional example, openly said that we were going to hire young children to handle toxic chemicals at low wages under appalling conditions in a foreign country where the intended markets were rapidly growing and the relevant laws were painfully weak, and then we went ahead, did exactly that, and made tons of money, we might claim that we had acted honestly, spoken truthfully, and kept our word, but we doubt that many people would consider us to be persons of high integrity. Personal integrity at the absolute base depends upon *an active and respectful consideration of the rights and well-being of others.*

But, how do we establish evaluative standards for this "active and respectful consideration of the rights and well-being of others?" As alluded to previously in this chapter, moral philosophers have—over millennia, not just centuries—developed a series of what they at the time considered to be universal (applicable to everyone), absolute (with exceptions for no one), impartial (without favoritism for any one), and basic (understandable by all) ethical principles that could logically be used to construct convincing arguments in favor of decisions and actions that could rationally be expected to contribute to what is now generally called the "common good." This common good, once again, can be defined as an *impartially* selected balance of the well-being and rights for all of the members within a full society, and thus can be said to be right and just and fair or—once again, our preferred term—legitimate. It would be legitimate in our view because it would be based upon economic efficiency, legal conformity, *and a set of generally accepted ethical principles, and their derived rules or standards.*

These generally accepted ethical principles are usually interpreted as normative commands as to what *must* be done to contribute impartially to the common good, and thus to be adjudged as right and just and fair.

But those outcome terms of rightness, justice, and fairness are indefinable, that common good balance of well-being and rights for the full society is immeasurable, and—lastly—many persons in managerial positions in for-profit, non-profit, and governmental positions object to being told what they *must* do beyond what economic efficiency suggests and legal conformity requires to be considered right and just and fair in their decisions and actions. We need a far more logically convincing means of applying the evaluative construct of personal integrity.

Suppose instead we look at these ethical principles for people in managerial positions whose decisions and actions can impact the well-being and rights of others *not as normative commands as to what must be done to be judged right and just and fair but as insightful suggestions as to what might be done to be lower the amount of conflict and increase the level of cooperation within society.* Lowering the amount of conflict and increasing the level of cooperation would obviously benefit everyone, not specific individuals, groups, or organizations within society, and would thus reinforce the impartiality of the decision process. With this demonstrated impartiality, the *intent* of the decision maker or makers could then be subjectively perceived, *not objectively adjudged,* as being right and just and fair—here we are using one more time these non-definable but frequently mentioned terms we don't like but have to occasionally employ to get our point across—by those impacted in either positive or negative ways by given managerial decisions or actions.

The subjective perception of a *just intent* in the decisions and actions by the managers of for-profit, non-profit, or governmental organizations among the persons who may well be impacted by those decisions and actions is one of the most basic motivational factors in all of the practice of management. We shall have far more to say about this perception of just intent in the final chapter of this book, and its motivational importance, but here we want to get back to considering ethical principles as insightful suggestions rather than normative commands.

Essentially, each of these insightful suggestions asks, "If you look at a proposed managerial decision or action, which you believe will result in a mixture of benefits and harms, and a contrast of rights recognized and rights ignored, for other individuals, groups, and organizations and thus has the potential to irritate some, cause conflict with others, and reduce the cooperation between many of the members of our society from the perspective of this ethical principle, would this perspective help you to change your mind or does it logically support your proposed decision or course of action?" That is a lengthy question, but it is a critical one. *It contains no normative demand that you must change your proposed course of action. There is only what we term an insightful suggestion that you think about changing that proposed course because lesser conflict and greater cooperation will clearly benefit you, your group, your organization, and your society.*

There are seven of these "insightful suggestions" that we believe help to remove the irritations that naturally occur within human beings when they feel that they are being treated in ways that they believe not to be right and just and fair, and that we judge not to be legitimate because they are not supported by a principle, rule, or standard that can logically be shown to be impartial between different individuals, groups, and organizations. We will list them here briefly in their historical sequence. All that we would like, as your read the seven entries in that sequence, is that you ask yourself, "Would this principle, rule, or standard, if followed universally, have a good chance of reducing the conflict between and improving the cooperation among the individuals, groups, and organizations that are associated with our organization?"

A description of the historical background, the name of the actual author, and an explanation of the supportive rationale for each of the entries within this sequence will be offered in chapter 5, complete with citations. Here we are going to exclude the authors and the citations because we want readers to consider the issues, not the sources. Both here and there we will list them as questions to emphasize the descriptive "maybe this will help you to personally decide" rather than the normative "here's what you must unquestionably do" focus that we much prefer, and we use current language and examples to try to convey the basic evaluative dimensions that are being proposed. Again, this will all be expanded further—with the historical context and the source citations—within chapter 5.

1. *Individual interests*: Does the decision or action that I and members of my group or organization are currently considering advance our long-term, enlightened self-interests, or may it over time damage those self-interests by ignoring the rights or harming the well-being of other individuals, groups, or organizations who later may ignore our rights or harm our well-being when they first find the opportunity?

2. *Personal virtues*: Does the decision or action that I and members of my group or organization are now considering damage the rights or harm

the well-being of other individuals, groups, or organizations and, if so, have we been open, honest, and truthful about those potential impacts, and would we feel proud and honored were those impacts to become widely known?

3. *Religious injunctions*: Is the decision or action that I and others of my group or organization are now considering one that is kind and compassionate toward other people, and does it create a sense of community, a belief that all of us are working jointly toward a common goal of peace between and well-being for all?

4. *Universal duties*: Is the decision or action that I and others in my group or organization are now considering one that treats all others as ends, worthy of dignity and respect, not as simple means to our own ends, and is it one that we would be willing to see all others free, able, and even encouraged to take?

5. *Combined rights and duties*: Is the decision or action that I and others in my group or organization are now considering one that recognizes the duality of rights and duties? That is, if we have a right to make this decision or take this action, do we have a concurrent duty that goes with that right, and does that duty improve the lives of others within our society?

6. *Distributive justice*: Does the decision or action that I and others in my group or organization are now considering avoid any negative impact upon the rights and well-beings of the least among us—those with the least income, education, wealth, skill, influence or power—so that they can continue to participate, at their current levels, in the output product and input resource markets?

7. *Contributive liberty*: Does the decision or action that I and others in my group or organization are now considering adequately take notice of the rights of everyone, not just the least among us, to develop their skills to the fullest so that they will be better able to arrange their voluntary exchanges in the output product and input resource markets as they see most fitting.

The basic problem with these seven ethical principles, whether used as: (a) normative commands as to what must be done to be adjudged right and just and fair; or (b) as insightful suggestions as to what might be done to decrease conflict and increase cooperation throughout our society, is that, once again, there is an underlying assumption. The underlying assumption for the evaluative construct of personal integrity is that the people involved in a given situation will react similarly to logical principles that bring impartiality into the character of the decider. But it has to be remembered that those people involved come from different economic and social situations and from different cultural and religious traditions, and thus they have different goals, norms, beliefs, and values and consequently different personal standards of proper or—once again, our preferred term—legitimate conduct.

In our view, all three of the evaluative constructs—economic efficiency, legal conformity, and personal integrity—have separate strengths and weaknesses, and a central responsibility of managers is to recognize the weaknesses—the underlying assumptions—and to apply the strengths—the mechanisms for impartiality—to managerial decisions and actions that have the potential to impact, in both positive and negative ways, the well-being and rights of other individuals, groups, and organizations within our society. *Separately these evaluative constructs have underlying weaknesses; together they offer an overriding strength.*

Conclusion to Chapter 2: Proposing the Solution

Any single chapter that attempts to describe the meaningful contributions and the underlying assumptions of economic efficiency, legal conformity, and personal integrity in a limited number of pages is going to appear crowded, detailed, perhaps just a bit confused and maybe even more than just a bit elementary. We wanted to introduce the major issues that we believe to be important in thinking about the nature and extent of managerial responsibility, about the nature and extend of *your* responsibility to other individuals, groups, organizations, and societies. What are those major issues? We believe that there are four of them, with the last one derived from the first three, and we've tried to express each in a personalized "do you agree with our understanding here?" format.

1. You have a balance of "to whom" responsibilities in all of your decisions and actions that include the organization at which you work, the society of which you are a member, and the person you are or want to become. However, no one can tell you what that balance ought to be. You have the ability—and, in our view, the duty—to decide for yourself.

2. You have a balance of "for what" responsibilities in all of your decisions and actions to search for outcomes that balance the standards of economic efficiency, legal conformity, and personal integrity Again, no one can tell you what that balance ought to be. Here also you have the ability—and, once more in our view, the duty—to decide for yourself.

3. But you also have to recognize that other people are going to differ with you in their judgments of those decisions and actions. People in a global economy come from different religious and cultural traditions and from different economic and social situations, they have different goals, norms, beliefs, and values, and thus different standards of proper conduct.

4. Consequently, you have the managerial responsibility to be prepared to present a logically convincing and legitimately supported argument in favor of the alternative you propose when the organization for which you work is considering a decision or action that in your view is contrary to your standards of proper conduct.

But, why should you and others do this? Why should people in managerial positions at for-profit, non-profit, and governmental organizations take the time and make the effort to form their own personal viewpoints on what they consider to be the most legitimate balance of the benefits and harms, and of the rights recognized and the rights ignored, for each of the of individuals, groups, organizations, and even societies impacted by a given organizational decision or action? And of even greater importance, why should they then decide to present that viewpoint to others within their organization, even though that presentation might not be well received by some of those others? We've all heard the expression "To get along, go along." Why not here? Our argument, and this will be expressed in the final chapter of this book, is that people who are rationally convinced about the *worth* of what they are doing simply do it better, with more trust, commitment, and cooperative/innovative effort. It is never possible to logically convince everyone. But it is possible to make the attempt when, in your view, you have logically balanced the "to whom part of your responsibilities to your self, your organization, and your society and the "for what" part of your responsibilities for economic efficiency, legal conformity, and personal integrity. Perhaps—and please consider this—given the changing conditions of the global economy where competition is fast becoming far more intense, technology far more complex, and cooperation/innovation far more essential, it is *worth* making that attempt for yourself, your organization, and your society.

Now, we move on to a more complete explanation of the known strengths and the inherent weaknesses of the evaluative construct of economic efficiency as will be detailed in chapter 3.

CHAPTER 3

Applying the Evaluative Construct of Economic Efficiency

The end of the housing boom in 2006, the start of the foreclosure process in 2007, and the near bankruptcy of the financial industry in 2008 were sequentially connected. The latter could not have happened without the former, and the resulting combination was one of the most destructive collapses ever to occur throughout the economy of the United States, and to some extent that of the world.

The *Final Report of the National Commission on the Causes of the Financial and Economic Crisis in the United States* prepared by the Financial Crisis Inquiry Commission (FCIC)[1] gave some dimensions to the destructiveness of this collapse. It explained that, in the late fall of 2010, just before that *Final Report* was sent to press, there were 26 million Americans who were out of work, could not find full-time work, or had given up looking for work. It continued that about 4 million American families had lost their homes to foreclosure, and another 4.5 million had slipped into the foreclosure process or were seriously behind on their mortgage payments. Lastly, it added that nearly $11 trillion in household wealth had vanished, with retirement accounts and life savings swept away.[2]

The harms were not all focused on individuals and families. Cities and towns had to provide help for long-term unemployed and protection for vacated properties as real estate tax revenues went down due to the sharp declines in property valuations. State and county governments faced similar shortages in their income tax and sales tax revenues, and had to lay off employees just as the need for those persons' services escalated.

Budget deficits at the federal level grew to unsupportable numbers, and a substantial part of the expanding deficit was caused by the need to pro-vided emergency funding for those local and state government units, plus additional capital for the nation's larger banks and investment houses that found themselves in danger of bankruptcy. On this issue, the Financial Crisis Commission concluded that "..., taxpayers had committed tril-lions of dollars through more than two dozen extraordinary programs to stabilize the financial system and to prop up the nation's largest financial institutions."[3]

Obviously, this was not a good period for the American society or the global economy. In our view, this happened not because of managerial selfishness and shortsightedness coupled with governmental neglect and delay, the usually named culprits, but because of competitive forces and technological advances that generated new products, markets, processes, and methods that in combination created rapidly changing conditions for the future that were not susceptible to the forms of managerial analysis developed for use in the past. It is difficult to decide what is the best or—using our awkward but much preferred term—most legitimate (meaning, let us explain one more time, "conforming to recognized principles or accepted rules or standards") thing to do when one does not know either the statistical probabilities or the financial values of the alternative future outcomes to many pending decisions and actions because of the rapidly changing conditions within both the society and the economy. The resi-dential housing market serves as a prime example of what can go inad-vertently but totally wrong under those rapidly changing and thus totally uncertain conditions.

Changes in the Residential Mortgage Industry

What had changed in the residential home mortgage industry that even-tually brought about this severe economic downturn and the resulting job losses, home foreclosures, local, state, and federal budget deficits, and financial industry bailouts? Just about everything! The changes here were even greater than those in the deepwater drilling industry that eventually—due to the same difficulty of applying unchanging forms of managerial analysis to rapidly changing conditions of the global economy—resulted in the destructive blowout, explosion, and fire on board the Deepwater Horizon at the Macondo well site as previously described in chapter 1.

In our view, there were three stages in the series of changes that took place in the residential home mortgage industry: the traditional, the innovative, and the exploitive. The differences between these stages were immense, and the time frames for adjustment were minute.

The traditional stage of the residential mortgage industry began with the start of middle income or retail-oriented commercial banking during the 1910s and the 1920s up to the aggressive expansion of those targeted services in the 1980s and the 1990s. Home mortgages during this period were essentially a contract between a married couple and a local bank. The couple wanted financing for an affordable house in a pleasant community as a place in which to raise their children, live their lives, and save for their retirement. The local bank, or the local office of a statewide bank, wanted a securely pledged asset (the physical house) and a solidly responsible couple with a steady income, a good credit record, and adequate savings or parental help for the required 20 percent down payment as a place in which to invest their capital.

Given those personal characteristics and those loan conditions, the default rates on traditional mortgages were almost non-existent, and home mortgages became known as extremely solid though somewhat stodgy bank investments with decent financial returns but only slight prospects for expansion. There simply were not enough married couples who met all three of the steady income, good credit, and 20 percent down payment requirements for a bank to rapidly expand this line of lending. Something new was needed to grow the business.

The innovative stage in the residential mortgage industry started during the early 1970s, and essentially can be credited to the ideas of a single entrepreneur. Angelo Mozilo, the principle founder and long-serving CEO of Countrywide Financial Corporation, provided the needed "something new." Mr. Mozilo had grown up in straightened circumstances in New York City. He was determined to improve himself, obtained a scholarship to Fordham, graduated with a degree in engineering, but then went to work as a commercial real estate salesman. It was a fortuitous choice. He related well with clients, focused on what they wanted rather than on what was available, and quickly became successful.

In 1972, Mr. Mozilo, together with an older friend who had specialized in real estate finance, formed the Countrywide Financial Corporation. This company did not sell commercial real estate in New York City; instead, they operated as a mortgage broker for real estate agents and prospective home buyers in the suburbs surrounding that city. In 1978, after hearing for years about the high growth rates in the suburbs surrounding Los Angeles, they moved their company to that area to participate in that growth. Again, it was a fortuitous choice. The company quickly became very successful.

The reasons for that success, Mr. Mozilo later explained, were really very simple. Countrywide Financial offered a range of innovative mortgage products that enabled large numbers of low- to middle-income families to purchase new homes both as better places for them to live and as secure investments for their future. The employment histories and the credit reports for the applicants had to be solid, but the size of the mortgage and the rate of the interest would vary with the level of income and the extent of debt. Those variations, coupled with the solid employment histories and good credit reports, made economic sense to most lenders, which meant that the completed mortgages were easy to place with local and statewide banks, despite the lack of the traditional down payments. Mr. Mozilo claimed that the rapidly rising prices for residential real estate in Southern California quickly brought the market determined value of each purchased home above the borrowed mortgage amount so that the need for down payments was no longer so important a consideration.

Originally, each mortgage was purchased individually by an area bank, but as the volume grew, Countrywide began to package them in groups with similar real estate characteristics, client income levels, and client credit scores upon which the banks could bid. These informal packages of residential mortgages with (a) known property characteristics; (b) confirmed borrower qualifications; and (c) competitive bid prices quickly caught the attention of Wall Street banks and investment firms. With those three characteristics, the growth truly began to escalate because large amounts of foreign capital had recently become available to those large banks and investment firms from high-income citizens in developing countries who wanted secure places in which to place their savings.

> The time tested 30-year fixed rate mortgage, with a 20 percent down payment, went out of style. There was a burgeoning global demand for residential mortgage-backed securities that offered seemingly solid and secure returns. Investors around the world clamored to purchase securities built on American real estate, seemingly one of the safest bets in the world.[4]

There was a widespread demand for these mortgage-backed securities, and not just from prosperous foreign investors. One of the few complimentary things that is still frequently said about Wall Street banks and investment firms is that they do tend to respond promptly to the market demands of their larger individual and corporate clients. At the start of this new line of business, those banks and investment houses purchased mortgages following what might be called the "West Coast" model as large packages with similar—and confirmed—property characteristics, borrower qualifications, and interest rates, packaged them as bonds, and then submitted those bonds essentially without change to the credit-rating agencies before sale to interested investors. Credit rating was fairly simple because of the known property specifications and borrower qualifications. It was true that no history of borrower performance over time existed for these new groups of low- to middle-income families whose property and payments provided the bond support. Usually this performance over time was the deciding matter in fixed-income credit ratings, but the rapidly rising price levels for the underlying assets (residential housing in growing sections of the prospering United States) made default appear highly unlikely. Credit agencies soon established a pattern of awarding the highly desired AAA ratings to these new and thought-to-be-very-solid mortgage-backed securities.

The use of subprime mortgage-backed securities soon spread throughout the country, beyond the originating states of California, Arizona, Nevada, and Florida. It appeared that a new financing method had been developed that provided investors with a decent return (interest rates considerably above US treasury bonds), excellent security (people's homes as the underlying asset), and diversified risk (multiple home owners in different occupations and at different life-cycle stages), and that this new bundling method could be applied to many other consumer and/or small business credit needs. Appearances, however, are often deceiving, and they certainly were in this instance.

> James Rokakis, the county treasurer of Cuyahoga County, where Cleveland was located, watched as home prices rose 66 percent from 1989 to 1999 and [then] bad lending practices enveloped the entire area. His statement to the Financial Crisis Inquiry Commission was: "Securitization was one of the most brilliant financial innovations of the twentieth century. It freed up a lot of capital. If it had been done responsibly, it would have been a wondrous thing because nothing is more stable, there's nothing safer, than the American mortgage market. It worked for years. But then people realized they could scam it."[5]

Problems in the Residential Mortgage Industry

And scam it they did. The exploitive stage of the residential mortgage market started in the late 1990s with the recognition that scamming was possible. It soon spread throughout all levels of the residential mortgage market, including the home buyers and home owners who now became more participants than customers in the residential mortgage market. Scamming, or the acceptance of scamming, then worked its way upward through the different levels of mortgage brokers, investment bankers, and rating agencies until it reached the security buyers in what had now clearly become a vertical value chain. The sales volumes and investment complexities expanded rapidly, and we will attempt to explain those changes at each of these relevant levels.

1. *Home buyers and home owners*: Both potential home buyers and existing home owners began to look at the continuing rise in house valuations as a certainty. Housing prices would always go up was the prevailing thought. Therefore, many home buyers did not intend to live in the house after they purchased it; instead they wanted to sell or "flip" it to another buyer after a year or two of price appreciation. Also, many existing home owners did not worry about repayment; rising home prices would always take care of that, they thought. Consequently, they took out additional loans upon their property, and used the money not for saving but for living. Through refinancing of this nature, Americans extracted $2.0 trillion in home equity between 2000 and 2007.[6]

   In an interview with the commission, Angelo Mozilo, the long-term CEO of Countrywide Financial—a lender brought down by its risky mortgages—said that a "gold rush" mentality overtook the country during these years, and that he was swept up in it as well: "Housing prices were rising so rapidly—at a rate that I'd never seen in my 55 years in the business—that people, regular people, average people got caught up in the mania of buying a house, and flipping it, making money. It was happening. They buy a house, make $50,000...and talk at a cocktail party about it. Housing suddenly went from being part of the American dream to house my family, to settle down. It became a commodity. That was a change in the culture...It was sudden, unexpected.[7]

2. *Mortgage brokers*: The mortgage brokers scurried to accommodate these new and eager customers. Subprime mortgages to low- and middle-income families already existed. They had been a major component of the innovative stage in the development of the housing mortgage industry, but then income levels and credit histories were rigorously verified. Now it was strictly a matter of "Tell us what you make, and how much you owe," and those answers were put down in

the proper spaces on the mortgage application form without question. This was the start of what was called "the liar loan."

> Paul McCulley, a managing director at PIMCO, one of the nation's largest money management firms, told the commission that he and his colleagues began to get worried... in 2005; they therefore sent out credit analysts to 20 cities to do what he called "old-fashioned shoe-leather research," talking to real estate brokers, mortgage brokers, and local investors about the housing and mortgage markets. They witnessed what he called "the outright degradation of underwriting standards.[8]

The mortgages themselves were no longer simple and direct agreements with set interest rates and known monthly payments. There were "adjustable rate" loans in which interest rates could be changed at the discretion of the lender. There were "teaser rate" loans, with unrealistically low rates offered for the first year or two that then suddenly escalated to above-market levels. There were "interest only" loans for a given period of time, but then the missed principle payments had to be quickly brought up to date. There were even "reverse amortization" loans in which the lender paid the borrower a given percentage of the home value for a short period or time before recovering that amount, and "mortgage amount greater than sales price" loans in which the lender pocketed that difference right at the start. It is alleged that borrowers were essentially told by their mortgage brokers, "Don't worry about these terms now; you can always refinance later, after the value of your house goes up and you can get better deals."[9]

The interest rates charged and the sales commissions paid by the mortgage brokerage firms on these "don't worry, you can always refinance later" loans were both far higher than on the "here's the amount of the mortgage now, here's the interest rate you'll pay for the duration of that mortgage, and here's the monthly payment you'll have to meet to pay off that mortgage in this number of years" type. The result was a widespread effort by sellers to convince buyers to take the "don't worry" type of home loans that the Financial Crisis Inquiry Commission later deemed to have been "predatory and fraudulent,"[10] and then almost immediately afterwards declared to have come from a total collapse of mortgage lending standards throughout the entire home mortgage value chain:

> [The] collapsing mortgage-lending standards and the mortgage securitization pipeline lit and spread the flame of contagion and crisis.[11]

Many mortgage lenders set the bar so low that lenders simply took eager borrowers' qualifications on faith, often with a willful disregard for a borrower's ability to repay. Nearly one quarter of all mortgages made in the first half of 2005 were interest-only loans. During the same year, 68 percent of "option ARM" [adjustable rate mortgage at the option of the lender] loans originated by Countrywide and Washington Mutual [a second very large mortgage broker that also eventually had to be rescued] had low or no-documentation requirements.[12]

At first, not a lot of people really understood the potential hazards of these new [interest only, adjustable rate, withdrawn equity] loans. They were new, they were different, and the consequences were uncertain. But it soon became apparent that what had looked like newfound wealth was a mirage based on borrowed money. Overall mortgage indebtedness in the United States climbed from $5.3 trillion in 2001 to $10.5 trillion in 2007.[13]

3. *Multiservice banks and investment firms*: The multiservice banks and large investment firms, primarily centered in New York City and with many actually headquartered on Wall Street itself, readily transformed these new, different, and undocumented home mortgages into new, different, and apparently credit-worthy financial instruments. There were three forms of these apparently credit-worthy financial instruments. We should like to emphasize that the following definitions apply only to those financial instruments constructed from residential mortgages, and that these definitions have been reduced to what we believe to be the basics to make their current functions and future problems more readily understandable.

- *Residential mortgage-backed securities (RMBS)*: A RMBS is a separate legal entity that has been constructed by a multiservice bank or investment firm to hold a pool of residential mortgages purchased from smaller local banks and/or brokers. The ownership of those residential mortgage assets is held within that legal entity, but the cash flows—that is, the monthly payments on the interest due and the balance reduction for each of the included mortgages—are received by the bank or investment firm but paid under contract to the purchaser of each portion of that legal entity. Any portions not sold to investors remain the holdings of the bank or investment firm that had formed and then divided the entity.

A simple example would be a legal entity that had been formed and financed by a large bank or investment firm, and then filled with purchased mortgages that, after adding their expenses, fees, and a profit margin, they valued at $100 million. These purchased mortgages as they came into the bank would commonly have different risk perceptions based upon: (a) the employment positions, income levels, and credit histories of the borrowers; and (b) the purchase prices, professional appraisals, or other sources for the valuations of the properties. The purchased mortgages would thus have different interest rates. The entire $100 million mortgage pool would next be vertically divided or "diced" into $10,000 bonds, each containing a range of credit histories, loan terms, perceived risks, and interest rates. The bonds would then be marketed to investors who preferred greater diversification in their holdings.

- *Collateralized debt obligations (CDO)*: These are essentially a different version of the first type of RMBS described above; those "diced" from an entity or pool that contained mortgages with a range of credit histories, loan terms, perceived risks, and interest rates. Here, however, the entity or pool was first organized into levels or "tranches" with mortgages having the highest perceived risks and highest interest rates in the bottom tranche, and then gradually working their way up to mortgages with the lowest risks and lowest rates in the tranche at the top. The pool was next divided horizontally, or "sliced," into tranches that held mortgages with similar rates and risks. Finally, each tranche was then cut horizontally, or—once again—"diced," into $10,000 bonds for sale to clients who wanted more specification in their holdings.

  We assume that readers have noticed the reason that—given the slicing and dicing that occurred—it later became so difficult to determine the actual holder of a residential mortgage after the owner of that residence defaulted on his/her mortgage.
- *Credit default swaps* (CDS): CDS are very different from the previously described RMBS and CDO forms. CDS are one type of a very large group of investment securities known as "derivatives." That is, the value of such a security was not dependent upon the value of an underlying asset pledged for its support, as in a home mortgage, a car loan, or a "short sale" (in which equities or bonds, frequently borrowed from their true holders, were pledged to support what was in reality a loan, not a sale). Instead, the value was "derived" from

similar but unpledged assets (similar homes, automobiles, equities, or bonds) and therefore had no support beyond the credit worthiness of the two parties (termed "counterparties") that negotiated the purchase or sale of such a "swap" in contract form. The simple way to think about derivatives is that neither the buyer nor the seller has to own the asset; they just have to be prepared—or, unfortunately, as it ultimately turned out, just have to just appear to be prepared—to fulfill the financial obligations of the contract.

The seller of one of these CDS contracts agreed to pay the buyer a set annual fee over the life of the contract, while the buyer agreed to pay the seller a set total amount if the derived value of the non-owned asset went down below a specified level. The latter is termed a "short" in financial parlance because if there had been an actual asset that was declining in value the holder would want to get out of the ownership as quickly as possible. The alternative is termed a "long" because, once again, if there were an actual asset that was rising in value the holder would want to continue ownership over the continuance of the price rise.

The "short" type of this arrangement is often compared to insuring against loss, but it is more hedging (establishing a counterbalance to an already established position) or speculating (literally betting on the expectation of the outcome, often with that expectation based not on personal intuition but upon extremely complex quantitative models of prospective future conditions). As long as the demand for and the price of residential housing continued to grow, there were plenty of long-position buyers, and as long as the credit worthiness of the purchased home mortgages continued to decline, there were a growing number of short-position sellers.

The securitization problem that later became apparent at the level of the multiservice banks and large investment firms—the producers and marketers of the RMBS, CDO, and CDS instruments—was that those banks and firms were far more aware of the steady decline in the credit worthiness of the home mortgages they had purchased from the mortgage brokers, and of the overoptimism of the credit reports they had obtained from the rating agencies, than were the investors who bought the mortgage-based securities the large banks and investment firms had constructed, but latter abandoned.

Goldman Sachs was one of the large banks and investment firms that had been investigated as a "case study" by the US Senate Permanent

Subcommittee on Investigations (SPSI). In their lengthy study titled Wall Street and the Financial Crisis: Anatomy of a Financial Collapse,[14] authors of the majority staff report explained in some detail that from 2004 to 2008 Goldman had constructed and then marketed 93 RMBS and 27 CDO securitizations with a total value approaching $100 billion, and built up its own multibillion dollar account of proprietary RMBS holdings. In December 2006, however, Goldman traders saw evidence that the untested mortgage loans with the non-confirmed borrower histories they had purchased, bearing the optimistic credit ratings they had encouraged, were beginning to show signs of the delinquencies and defaults they had expected:

> Goldman quietly and abruptly reversed course...Over the next two months, it rapidly sold off or wrote down the bulk of its existing subprime RMBS and CDO inventory and began building a short [CDS] position that would allow it to profit from the decline of the mortgage market. Throughout 2007, Goldman twice built up and then cashed in sizeable mortgage related short positions. At its peak, Goldman's net short position totaled $13.9 billion. Overall in 2007, its net short position produced record profits totaling $3.7 billion for Goldman's Structured Products Group...
>
> Throughout 2007, Goldman sold RMBS and CDO securities to its clients without disclosing its own net short position against the subprime mortgage market or its purchase of CDS contracts to gain from the loss in value of some of the very securities it was selling to its clients.[15]

4. *Rating agencies*: The rating agencies—Moody's and Standard and Poor are the major ones—have been strongly condemned for not rigorously examining the credit worthiness of the purchased home mortgages or—for that matter—even considering the eventual limit of the housing market boom. But, in their defense, it has to be admitted that they were evaluating a surprisingly large number of innovative securities based upon traditionally solid family housing assets and submitted by apparently reliable Wall Street clients during a period of encouraging economic well-being throughout the United States:

> Between 2004 and 2007, Moody's and S&P issued credit ratings for tens of thousands of U.S. residential mortgage backed securities (RMBS) and collateralized debt obligations (CDO). Taking in

increasing revenue from Wall Street firms, Moody's and S&P issued AAA and other investment grade ratings for the vast majority of these RMBS and CDO securities, deeming them safe investments even though many relied upon high risk home loans.[16]

Part of the coming problem, of course, was the long-standing nature of the client relationships that existed between the multiservice banks and investment firms that had developed and then produced the new RMBS and CDO securities, and the smaller but essential credit rating firms that provided the needed high-grade approvals, and were well paid by those same banks and firms for doing so. But the problem, when it did come, was much larger than anyone had ever conceived:

> Traditionally, investments holding AAA ratings have had a less than one percent probability of incurring defaults. But in 2007, the vast majority of RMBS and CDO securities with AAA ratings incurred substantial losses; some failed outright. Analysts have determined that over 90 percent of the AAA ratings given to subprime RMBS securities originating in 2006 and 2007 were later downgraded by the rating agencies to junk status.[17]

5. *Final customers*: The last step or level in this vertical value chain from home buyers to mortgage brokers to investment banks to rating agencies was to the final customers—both individual and institutional—who bought the RMBS and CDO securities, some already internally hedged by their sellers with CDS derivatives that they—the sellers—retained. It can be alleged that the final customers should have performed better due diligence, but perhaps even the best of due diligence could not have anticipated the problems that were coming:

> The nation's financial system had become vulnerable and interconnected in ways that were not understood by either the captains of finance or the system's public stewards. In fact, some of the largest institutions had taken on what would prove to be debilitating risks. Trillions of dollars had been wagered on the belief that housing prices would always rise and that borrowers would seldom default on mortgages, even as their debt grew. Shaky loans had been bundled into investment products in ways that seemed to give investors the best of both worlds—high yield and risk free—but instead, in many cases, would prove to be high risk and yield free.[18]

What was the eventual outcome of this series of misinformed decisions and misappropriate actions by home buyers, mortgage brokers, investment bankers, credit raters, and final investors? The Financial Crisis Inquiry Commission reported that by June 2008 the total value of mortgage-backed securities issued and sold between 2001 and 2006 had reached $13.4 trillion.[19] This was a huge figure, slightly above the full governmental debt of the United States ($13.2 trillion), that caused such economic concern and political stress throughout the spring and summer of 2011. And, as has been described before, much of this $13.4 trillion of mortgage-backed debt had improper ratings, incredible complexity, and problematic value. Essentially, the vertical value chain of the residential housing/mortgage industry was a stack of unstable blocks, ready to fall. And fall they did, far and hard.

We have tried to recount the rapid change of the residential mortgage industry across the three stages of traditional, innovative, and exploitive, and through the five levels of home buyers, mortgage brokers, investment banks, credit rating agencies, and final investors, *without ascribing blame.* It would have been easy to ascribe blame, given the apparent shortsightedness and obvious self-centeredness of many of the managerial decisions and actions within four of those five levels—the final buyers were the exception; they were the victims, not the perpetrators—in the residential mortgage value chain.

There was also plenty of blame outside of those four of the five levels of profit progression within the residential mortgage value chain that could easily have been placed on the backs of federal agencies. Certainly the Housing and Urban Development Department's policies to encourage home ownership through various incentives and supports played a part. Certainly the Federal Reserve's decisions to rely on competitive market forces rather than to impose prudent mortgage standards played a part. Certainly the Securities and Exchange Commission's decisions to permit thin capital reserves and to allow massive short-term borrowings played a part. And lastly, certainly the US Congress's replacement of the Glass-Steagall Act of 1933, which had long separated investment banking (equities and capital gains) from commercial banking (loans and interest payments), with the Gramm-Lech-Bliley Act of 1999, which abruptly removed those loans versus equity distinctions, played a very major part.

This is in the nature of an aside, but the authors of the Financial Crisis Inquiry Commission report continually refer to the commingling of the investment banking and commercial banking functions, which soon occurred following the repeal of the 1930s depression era legislation, as a "shadow banking system." We much prefer the term "multiple service banking industry" because this group of large and complex financial institutions *was not a shadow.* It was offering multiple services, well out in the open, from very large and highly visible office structures.

This also is in the nature of an aside, but one of the staff assigned to writing the preface to the Financial Crisis Inquiry Commission report had quoted the testimony by the chief executive officer at one of those large and complex multiservice banks, doubtless situated in one of these large and highly visible office structures, that "a $40 billion position in highly rated mortgage securities would not in any way have excited my attention"; and then added his or her brief but acute observation: "In this instance, too big to fail meant too big to manage."[20]

Overlooking Problems in the Residential Mortgage Industry

But, getting back to the main theme of this chapter, we believe it is more important to understand how this total collapse of the residential mortgage industry and this near bankruptcy of the multiservice banking industry actually occurred than attempt to ascribe blame. Why did home buyers and home owners sign exploitive mortgage contracts, in many instances knowing that they could not make the payments? Why did mortgage brokers sell those likely-to-fail mortgage contracts to large banks and investment firms knowing of their lack of confirmed documentation and thus of their increase of payment uncertainty rather than of payment risk? Why did the multiservice banks and investment firms package those undocumented and uncertain mortgages into complex financial instruments for sale to both individual and institutional investors, while at the same time establishing "short" positions in anticipation of a sharp decline in the value of the financial instruments they were then constructing, promoting, and marketing? Why did the credit rating agencies provide such solid endorsement of the end products of this process, apparently without any investigation of the underlying conditions? And lastly, why did the final customers—the individual and institutional investors—purchase those end products without themselves—or their inevitably well-paid advisors—looking for the clear-in-the-aftermath flaws that were obviously part of the process though not apparent in the product?

One of the standard answers to this "how did this happen" question is the assertion that the eventual disastrous aftermath of the rapid residential mortgage industry growth simply could not have been anticipated.

Charles Prince, the former chairman and chief executive officer of Citigroup Inc., called the collapse in housing prices "wholly unanticipated". Warren Buffett, the chairman and chief executive officer of Berkshire Hathaway Inc., which until 2009 was the largest single shareholder of Moody's Corporation, told the Commission that "very, very few people could appreciate the bubble," which he called a "mass delusion shared by "300 million Americans." Lloyd Blankfein, the chairman and chief executive officer of Goldman Sachs Group, Inc. likened the financial crisis to a hurricane.

Regulators echoed a similar refrain. Ben Bernanke, the chairman of the Federal Reserve Board since 2006, told the Commission a "perfect storm" had occurred that regulators could not have anticipated…Alan Greenspan, the Fed chairman during the two decades leading up to the crash, told the Commission that it was beyond the ability of regulators to ever foresee such a sharp decline.[21]

Still, there were people who did foresee the coming financial disaster, and tried to warn others. James Rokakis, the county treasurer of Cuyahoga County, where Cleveland is located, has been quoted earlier in this chapter in his testimony to the Financial Crisis Inquiry Commission that he had greatly favored mortgage securitization when he first heard of it as a process to help home buyers and revitalize city neighborhoods, "but then people realized they could scam it."[22]

They certainly did scam it. Mr. Rokakis explained that he had found, in his position as county treasurer, that unsafe mortgage loans and poor lending practices had become standard practice throughout the Cleveland area. He continued that he had tried to warn officials of the Federal Reserve attending a conference in Cleveland about the local situation, and went on to ask them to issue new mortgage lending rules to deal with the situation. Nothing happened. Mr. Rokakis concluded his testimony by saying, "I naively believed they'd go back and tell Mr. Greenspan and presto, we'd have some new rules…It [that expectation] was kind of quaint."[23]

This report of problems in the residential mortgage industry, with an expectation of a change in the rules and a disappointment in the results, quickly became a common experience. A group of state attorney generals who attempted to stop what they viewed as extensive mortgage frauds within their jurisdictions were told by the Office of the Controller of the Currency in very harsh terms that they should not attempt "to control the consumer practices of federally regulated institutions."[24] A real estate appraiser in Bakersfield, California, had studied the market, and found that many homes had higher mortgage loans than sales prices, which permitted insiders to skim money from each sale. He called a number of mortgage loan brokers and found that they did not seem to care. One even told him, "Don't put your nose where it doesn't belong."[25]

The concerns and complaints quickly moved up the ladder, from the lower rungs where market participants talked to regulatory staff members to the higher levels where consumer advocates and academic researchers addressed senior officials and central bankers. Ruhi Maker, a lawyer who worked as a consumer advocate on foreclosure cases at the Empire Justice Center in Rochester, New York, told Fed governors Ben Bernanke, Susan Bies, and Roger Ferguson who were present at a public hearing of the Consumer Advocacy Council that she suspected that some investment banks—she specified Bear Stearns and Lehman Brothers with an amazing degree of prescience—were securitizing such bad loans that the very survival of those firms was in question. "We repeatedly see false appraisals and false incomes," she explained to the Fed officials, and urged them to prod the Securities and Exchange Commission to toughen their mortgage lending requirements otherwise "serious questions could arise about whether they [those two investment banks, one of which did require rescue and the other one of which did go into bankruptcy] could be forced to buy back bad loans they had made or securitized."[26] She also was deeply disappointed at the reaction to her complaint:

> In an interview with the FCIC, Ms. Maker said that Fed officials seemed impervious to what the consumer advocates were saying. The Fed governors politely listened and said little, she recalled. They had their economic models, and their economic models did not see this coming, she said. We kept getting back, "This is all anecdotal."[27]

Anecdotal evidence is often downplayed in the basic social sciences such as economics, which for over 100 years have been increasingly built upon quantitative data, not personal observations, but even the early efforts to quantitatively support such personal observations within the increasingly troubled residential mortgage industry were widely disregarded. In August 2005, a meeting of invited (i.e., senior) economists was held at the Jackson Lake Lodge, a conference center located in one of the scenic valleys of the Grand Teton National Park in Wyoming. It was a "who's who of central bankers" said one of the attendees.[28]

Raghuram Rajan, who was then on leave from the University of Chicago's business school while he was serving as chief economist for the

International Monetary Fund, presented a paper titled "Has Financial Development Made the World Riskier?" The theme of the presentation was that managers throughout the residential mortgage industry were being exceedingly well compensated for their short-term gains but that they probably would not be held responsible for any eventual long-term losses because of: (a) the sequential nature of the value chain process (it would be hard to identify which individual or firm within that sequence had made the errors that would lead to the losses); and (b) the complex nature of the securities (it would even be more difficult to decide which individual or firm at the time of that loss actually owned the specific portions of the sliced and diced securities that had suffered those losses). Prof. Rajan was particularly concerned that the derivative-based credit default swaps had such a large denominational value that the financial system might become destabilized and the regulatory structure be unable to deal with the fallout. His paper was not well received:

> He recalled to the FCIC that he was treated with scorn. Lawrence Summers, a former U.S. treasury secretary who was then president of Harvard University called Rajan a "Luddite", implying that he was opposed to technological change. "I felt like an early Christian who had wandered into a convention of half-starved lions."[29]

Susan Wachter, a professor of real estate and finance at the University of Pennsylvania, got the same reception at a similar conference also held at the Jackson Lake Lodge two years later. She proposed that, due to the relaxed lending standards and complex mortgage securitizations, the United States might have a real estate crisis similar to that suffered in Asia in the 1990s. "It was universally panned," she later said, and an economist from the Mortgage Bankers Association called it "absurd."[30]

Lastly, Kyle Bass, a Dallas-based hedge fund manager and a former Bear Stearns executive testified before the FCIC that he had told senior people at the Federal Reserve that housing prices had reached excessive levels, and therefore the mortgage securitization products based upon those reputed values were in danger. "Their answer at the time..., and this was also the thought that was homogeneous throughout Wall Street, was that home prices always track income growth and job growth, and said 'We don't see what you're talking about because incomes are still growing and jobs are still growing.'"[31] His response essentially argued that the easy placement of mortgage-based securities was the driving force behind the easy issuance of shaky mortgages, which led to the easy sale of homes at unsustainable prices. They were claiming exactly the opposite, he concluded, that "in their view the tail [home prices] was wagging the dog [mortgage securities]."[32]

Reasons for Overlooking the Problems in the Residential Mortgage Industry

Why did this happen? Why did the local and regional managers who were actively engaged throughout the five levels of the residential mortgage industry, the senior officials and staff members at the numerous governmental agencies who were allegedly supervising those activities, and the academic researchers who were hopefully studying those individual, company, industry, and government interactions, all ignore the warnings that seemingly were so explicit and the evidence that apparently was so easily obtainable through observation?

Let us support this "easily obtained through observation" claim. Remember the previously cited managing director at PIMCO who sent out a few credit analysts to do what he termed "old-fashioned, shoe-leather research" by interviewing real estate sellers, mortgage brokers, and local investors in 20 different cities and found what he termed an outright degradation of lending standards. Others could have done exactly the same thing, but apparently no one did. Why not? There were in our view three reasons:

1. *"Cooperate and accept" culture*: The first reason, in our view, was the unusually cooperative nature of the five level structure—from home buyers to mortgage brokers to multiservice bankers to credit raters to final investors—of the residential mortgage industry in which each level contributed a specialized function to eventually generate a common end product and—as it turned out—a common end disaster. Chapter 1 explained that there were two types of these inherently cooperative industry structures that often were formed in response to high levels of both technological innovation and competitive intensity and a resultant widely felt need for reactive speed to apply that innovation, overcome that intensity, and make greater profits. These types were horizontal joint ventures and vertical value chains. We shall not repeat their definitions here. They are available in chapter 1.

   Chapter 1 went on to argue that people who were working together on a shared product, process, or project, but were employed by different companies and with different job skills, different knowledge bases, different experience levels, different risk perceptions, different performance measures, and different incentive systems would almost inevitably develop a widespread attitude of cooperation and acceptance with which they felt jointly comfortable. By "acceptance" within these increasingly common cooperative endeavors we explained that we meant a general feeling of "Well, I may not really like what you are doing, or plan to do, but you know more about your part of this joint venture or value chain in which we are working than I do, and if I object it will just bring our highly profitable and socially beneficial effort to an end so go ahead and we'll adjust." "We'll adjust" in the case of the residential mortgage value chain meant, "We'll do exactly what you're doing, and also make a lot more money too."

2. *"It can't happen here" syndrome*: Frequently in these highly cooperative efforts and advanced technological ventures, a general feeling develops that the innovations in products, processes, and methods that have brought about an explosion in growth have also brought about a reduction in risk. As recounted in chapter 2, the widespread attitude in the deepwater drilling joint venture was that, given the modern drilling platforms, the overlapping safety systems, and the intensified training efforts, a destructive blowout, explosion, and fire simply could no longer happen on an exploratory well site within the Gulf of Mexico. And, as was recounted in the early parts of this chapter, it was thought that the combination of innovative mortgage types, expanding subprime markets, the secure experiences with earlier pledged housing assets and the ready sales of the RMBS and CDO bonds, nothing could go wrong here either. Why, in both of those instances—in deepwater well drilling and in residential mortgage securitizing—did so many people ignore the facts?

3. *Assumptions of economic theory*: Now we get down to the basics. Why did so many well-trained and fully competent individuals overlook what now seem in retrospect to have been so obvious. We believe that those well-trained and fully competent individuals were not so much ignoring the facts; they were more forgetting the assumptions.

Almost all of the governors of the Federal Reserve Board, and many of the senior officials and mid-level staff in the Office of the Controller of the Currency and of the Securities and Exchange Commission, have a solid background in economic theory. That solid background is needed. It allows the governors, senior officials, and mid-level staff members to understand the complex interrelationships between global positions, federal policies, industry structures, corporate actions, and supplier/customer reactions.

But sometimes that solid background can lead people astray. It certainly did in the multiple instances we have recounted when participants in or researchers of the residential mortgage value chain reported: (a) the poor quality of the underlying mortgage loans; (b) the growing number of adverse credit default swaps; and (c) the unsustainable level of residential property prices.

In each of those multiple instances we have recounted, well-trained and presumably knowledgeable economists in responsible positions totally disregarded the predictions—each of which turned out to be uncannily accurate—of active participants in, or acknowledged researchers of, the residential mortgage industry. Why did this happen? In our view, there are some commonly acknowledged but frequently neglected assumptions that are part of the base of economic theory, and that "frequent neglected" aspect brought about the dismissive rejections of the accurate warnings.

Assumptions at the Base of Economic Theory

Economic theory is an empirically based social science with a proud history of development and a large number of active adherents in governmental, managerial, and academic positions. It is divided into two closely interrelated portions. The first is microeconomics, which focuses on how decisions are made and actions are taken by individuals, groups, and organizations throughout society that affect both: (a) the demand for and the supply of output goods and services; and (b) the demand for and supply of input material, labor, and capital. The prices for each are determined at the intersections of demand and supply through impartial "we don't care who comes out on top" market forces. The second is macroeconomics, which deals with how decisions are made and actions are taken by governmental institutions at the national, regional, and local levels that attempt to address such collective outcomes as growth rates, employment numbers, welfare needs, business cycles, and inflations trends that are also, of course, influenced by those impartial market forces.

We are interested in the first—microeconomics—which essentially deals with the efficiency of the productive system. True economic efficiency—the greatest production of the most-wanted goods and services at the smallest usage of the least wanted labor, material, and capital resources—produces not just profits for companies but also satisfactions for consumers, wages for workers, salaries for managers, dividends for owners, payments to suppliers, commissions to distributors, and benefits for societies. This broader sense of economic efficiency provides a solid evaluative principle, standard, or rule for the decisions and actions of managers that impact, both positively and negatively, the well-being and the rights of others. It is this broader sense that is critical, and we have termed this evaluative principle, standard, or rule "economic efficiency," because we want to emphasize the breadth of the outcome, not the precision of the theory.

For many people, the use of the construct of economic efficiency as a solid evaluative measure for the decisions and actions of managers that impact the well-being and rights of others in ways that are both positive and negative *seems an outright error in thinking.* They view the underlying theory as a mathematical approach to markets, prices, and outputs—devoid of all broader substance—that focuses solely on profit maximization. Members of this group, almost all of whom are non-economists, consider the theory of the firm to be descriptive, designed to rationalize the behavior of business managers as they attempt to maximize the long-term value of their firms, while paying scant attention to the environmental damages, product dangers, workplace risks, or similar "harmful to others" or "destructive of rights" impacts those managers may cause along the way.

There is no question but that over-concentration on profits for one's employer have resulted, throughout history, in environmental damages, product dangers, workplace risks, and similar negative outcomes. But, this is neither a consequence nor a corollary of the microeconomic theory that underlies our proposed principle, standard, or rule of economic efficiency. Economic theory, in its more complete form, is more a normative theory of society than a descriptive theory of business. We realize that we're not saying anything new here, but please bear with us. We're trying to get an answer to the question why numerous groups of unquestionably distinguished economists "got it wrong" in regards to a major social and financial problem: the destruction of the residential housing and mortgage securitizing industries, and the telling impact of that destruction upon the overall economy and society of the United States.

The central focus of the normative microeconomic theory of society is the efficient utilization of material, labor, and capital resources to satisfy consumer wants and needs. At economic equilibrium—and an essential element in reaching equilibrium throughout the entire microeconomic system is the effort by business managers to balance marginal increases in revenues against marginal increases in costs, which automatically results in maximum profits for the firm within market and resource constraints—it is theoretically possible to achieve a condition known as Pareto Optimality.

We assume now that we've reached this stage of the discourse on why so many distinguished economists "got it wrong" on the residential mortgage crisis that many of our readers are saying to themselves, "Everybody knows this; why start here?" Our argument in reply is that evaluative constructs—to be logically convincing—have to be universal (applicable to everyone), absolute (with exceptions for no one), impartial (without favoritism for any one), and basic (understandable by all). It is this latter "understandable by all" element that has been left out of the evaluative construct of economic efficiency, and so we want to explain the societal benefits of that efficiency very briefly but very basically.

Pareto Optimality refers to a condition in which the least wanted resources of society are: (a) accumulated so efficiently from competitive—and therefore impartial—input factor markets; (b) converted so efficiently by profit optimizing productive firms into the most wanted goods and services by society; and then these goods and services are (c) distributed so efficiently by the competitive—and therefore impartial—output product markets; that (d) it would be impossible to make any single person better off without harming some other person. Remember this phrase: "It would be impossible to make any single person better off without making some other person worse off." This trade-off is the evaluative principle, standard, or rule of economic efficiency encapsulated in the Pareto Optimality construct: produce the maximum economic benefits for society, recognizing the full personal and social harms of that production, and then broaden the receipt of those benefits and change the allocation of those harms, if it is widely believed to be truly needed, by democratic political decisions rather than economic market actions.

Doubtless the following explanation of the structural components and market relationships that result in these Pareto Optimal outcomes will be dull for all those with a reasonable understanding of economic theory, and perhaps trying for some of the others. But this explanation is necessary to show the *interdependencies between individuals, companies, and societies that are guided by impartial markets,* and thus can provide a non-biased evaluative principle, rule, or standard for the managerial decisions and actions that benefit some while harming others, or advance the rights of some while denying the rights of others. These market-based interdependencies between individuals, companies, and societies are shown graphically in

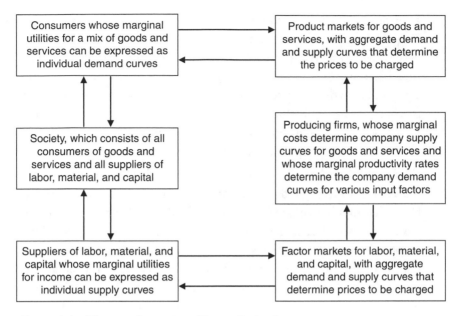

Figure 3.1 Theoretical structure of Pareto Optimal outcomes.

figure 3.1, which is followed by an explanation of each of the six cells in that graphic.

1. *Individual consumers*: Each consumer has a different set of preferences for the various goods and services that are available, and these preferences can be expressed as "utilities," or quantitative measures of the usefulness of a given product or service to a specific customer. The "marginal utility," or extra usefulness, of one additional unit of that product or service to that customer tends to decline with purchases, for eventually that person will have a surfeit of the good. The price that the person is willing to pay for the good also declines along with the marginal utility or degree of surfeit. The price relative to the number of units that will be purchased by a given person at a given time forms what is known as the individual demand curve.

   Price can also be used to compare the relative usefulness of different goods and services to an individual. It can be expected that a person selecting a mix of products will choose an assortment of goods and services such that marginal utility per monetary unit would be equal for all the items at a given level of spending for this individual. Each good would be demanded up to the point where the marginal utility per dollar would be exactly the same as the marginal utility per dollar for any other good. If a customer had a higher marginal utility relative to price for any particular good, he or she would doubtless substitute more of that good for some of the others to achieve a better balance among his or her preferences. The final balance or mix, where the marginal utilities per monetary unit are equal for all products and services, can be termed the point of equilibrium for that customer. It is also the point of optimal satisfaction for that customer; he or she is being optimally satisfied in the purchase of goods and services, up to the limit of his or her spendable income.

2. *Product markets*: A product market consists of all of the individual customers for a given good or service, together with all the producing firms that supply that good or service. The demand curves of all those customers can be aggregated to form a market demand curve. This market demand curve reflects the total demand for a good or service, relative to price. If the price in dollars is the vertical axis and demand in units the horizontal axis, the market demand curve will generally slope down and toward the right, indicating increasing customer demand as the purchase price declines, until all customers reach the point of surfeit. This certainly makes sense. People will buy more of what they most want and have the money to purchase, until they have enough, as the price goes down.

   Crossing this market demand curve is a market supply curve that portrays the total available supply, again relative to price. The market supply curve generally slopes upward and toward the right, for the higher the price, the more units in total most companies can be expected to produce, until all producers reach the limit of their capacity. The market price, of course, is set at the intersection of those two curves representing aggregate demand and aggregate supply. *This then is the point at which all customers are being optimally satisfied, up to the limit of their spendable incomes, and at which all firms are being optimally satisfied, up to the limit of their production capabilities.*

3. *Producing firms*: The aggregate supply curve, the "other half" of each product market relationship described above, is formed by adding together the individual supply curves of all of the producing firms. These individual supply curves are generated by the cost structures of those firms at different levels of production, while the actual level of production for each firm is determined by a comparison of "marginal revenues" and "marginal costs."

   The marginal revenue of a producing firm is the extra revenue that the firm would receive by selling one additional unit of the good or service. To sell that additional unit in a fully price-competitive market, it is necessary to move down the aggregate demand curve to a slightly lower price level. To sell that additional unit in a non-price-competitive market, it is necessary to spend greater amounts on advertising and/or promotion to differentiate the product from those manufactured by other firms. Under either alternative, the marginal revenue from selling the last unit will be less than the average revenue from selling all other units. Marginal revenues inevitably decrease with volume.

The marginal cost of the producing firm is the obverse of the marginal revenue. Marginal cost is the extra expense that the firm would incur by producing one additional unit of the product or service. Marginal costs initially decline with volume due to economies of scale and learning curve effects, but then eventually rise due to diminishing returns as the physical capacity of the plant is approached. The rising portion of the marginal cost curve forms the supply curve of the firm; it represents the number of units that the firm should produce and supply to the market at each price level.

The producing firm achieves equilibrium when marginal costs are equal to marginal revenues. At the intersection of the marginal cost and marginal revenue curves, the profits of the firm are maximized. Allegedly, the firm can increase profits only by improving its technology; this would change the marginal costs and consequently the supply curve. However, over the long term, it is assumed that all firms would adopt the new technology and achieve the same cost structure. Production equilibrium would thus be reestablished at the new intersections of the marginal cost and marginal revenue curves for all firms within the industry. *This is the point at which all firms are balancing their marginal revenues and their marginal costs, and therefore the point of greatest profits for all firms and greatest satisfactions for all managers at those firm producing competitive goods or services within a given industry.*

4. *Factor markets*: The technology of the producing firm determines the maximum output of goods and services that can be achieved for a given mix of input factors. The input factors of production are material (from basic raw materials to finished ready-to-install components), labor (from manual to conceptual), and capital (from debt to equity). Charges for these *productive* input factors are classified as direct expenses, and include costs for the materials, wages for the labor, and charges for the capital. These expenses are said to be

interdependent because the factors are interrelated; that is, one factor can be substituted for another in the production function.

The relationships among these input factors, and the amount of one that would have to be used to substitute for another, are determined by the technology of the production function and by the "marginal productivity" of each factor for a given technology. The marginal productivity of a factor of production is the additional output generated by adding one more unit of that factor while keeping all others constant. For example, it would be possible to add one additional worker to speed up a production line without changing the capital investments in the line or the material components of the product. There should then be an increase in the physical output of that production line, and that increase, measured in units or portions of units, would be the marginal productivity of that additional worker. To maximize profits, a company should increase the use of each factor of production until the value of its marginal productivity (the increase in unit output times the market price less any discounts, commissions, et cetera of those units) equals the cost of the input factor.

The market demand for each factor (material, labor, or capital) of production from all producing firms can be seen as a curve sloping downward from left to right for the lower the price the more of that factor will be substituted. The market supply for each factor of production from all individual suppliers can be seen as a curve sloping upward from the left to the right for the higher the price the more of that factor will be supplied. The market price is, of course, set at the intersection of those two curves. *This is the point at which all producing firms are being optimally satisfied up to the limit of their productive capabilities, and at which all individual suppliers are being optimally satisfied up to the limit of their disposable resources (labor, material, and money).*

5. *Individual suppliers:* The aggregate demand for each input supply factor of production is equal to the proportion of that factor used in the productive function of each firm times the total output in units of all firms that have been actively engaged in meeting the output product market demand. The demand for each input factor of production is therefore "derived" from the output markets for goods and services.

The aggregate supply of each factor of production, however, is limited by the hesitation of each owner to part with his or her factor. The supply of labor, for example, is limited by the hesitation of individual workers to work more than a personally determined number of hours on the job. This creates what is known as a backward sloping supply curve: each worker has a marginal utility for income that gradually decreases and becomes negative as his or her desire for greater leisure exceeds his or her preference for further income. The same effect can be seen, during period of general prosperity, on the supplies and hence on the prices of both investment capital and raw material. Most owners of capital make a new investment only if their utility for the projected return of the new investment exceeds their utility for the existing return from an old investment or for the cash reserves they hold. Most owners of raw materials—many of which involve land in one form or another: farming, logging, mining, drilling, developing, et cetera—sell that resource only if their utility for the income from that sale exceeds their utility for the continued possession and/or preservation of the resource. In short, and this is a major point we wish to convey in this discussion, owners of the factors of production sell the factors—time, money, or property—they least want to keep through input factor markets in order to garner the income to purchase the goods and services they most want to posses through the output product markets. *This equilibrium, of utility for income versus utility for possession, is the point of optimal satisfaction for the suppliers of material, labor, and capital up to the limit of their owned resource.*

6. *Complete society*: The owners of the factors of production, needed by the productive functions at various firms, are also the customers for the products and services generated by the productive functions at those various firms. The factor owners receive the rents (an obsolete term, referring to the ownership of land, the most basic material), the labor wages, and the interest/dividend/capital gain payments for the use of the resources they decide to sell or loan, following their personal preferences (utilities) for the resources they least want to keep, and then they purchase the goods and services they decide to buy, following their personal preferences (utilities again) for the products they most want to possess at the level of income they receive.

The customers for the output products are also the suppliers of the input factors. Together they include everybody—or almost everybody; the unemployed are excluded during their period of unemployment—within society. And so, when we talk about what is best for society, we are really talking about what is best for *all* of the individual participants within the economic system as determined by impartial market forces, except for the unemployed who theoretically will be compensated through political decisions rather than by market choices. This is the rationale for the Pareto Optimal outcome in which profit maximization for companies within market constraints leads to benefit maximization for all societal members as determined by the impartial structure of the twin input supply and output product markets. *In short, the circle is complete, from individual customers who chose for their own well-being to productive companies that chose for their own well-being to individual suppliers who chose for their own well-being to the societal well-being that results from that sequence of individual choices by everyone (except for the unemployed who are to be made whole by political choice) within society.*

Problems in the Application of Economic Efficiency

It would appear that the managers employed by the different companies working cooperatively in the horizontal joint venture of drilling an exploratory deepwater oil well within the Gulf of Mexico, both those on board the Deepwater Horizon and those on shore in the offices of those various companies, all followed Pareto Optimal decision processes in which profit maximization within the impartial constraints of the input supply and output product markets should have led to benefit maximization for all citizens. But, here it led to small gains in revenues and minor reductions in costs for the involved companies, and to truly massive financial and environmental harms (said to total over $20 billion at the time this manuscript was being prepared)[33] and to three of the most basic abridgements of human rights (the right to life, the right to health as a condition of that life, and the right to chose the type of life an individual might want and could afford) for everyone else. Something was dramatically wrong with the economic efficiency reasoning process here.

It would also appear that the managers employed by the different companies working cooperatively in the vertical value chain of providing residential mortgages to low- and middle-income families made use of the same Pareto Optimal decision processes in which profit maximization under input supply and output product market constraints should have led to benefit maximization for all citizens. But here, the outcome was even worse. There were large-scale bonus payments and profit gains for some, but huge financial losses (said to total over $11 trillion at the time of writing),[34] enormous home foreclosures (expected to reach 9 million),[35] and unstoppable employment declines (unemployment was above 9 percent three years after the onset of the housing crisis[36]) for everyone else. Something was again drastically wrong with the reasoning process in this instance.

What went wrong in these two memorable examples? Our belief is that the assumptions underlying the Pareto Optimal outcomes of economic theory were forgotten. Everyone knew them. They'd been around for years. But they were so well known that it seemed sophomoric for anyone to bring them up in discussion or debate. There are three of these conceptually important but easily bypassed requirements for managerial decisions and actions that are necessary to consider if managerial decisions and actions are to actually result in outcomes that are truly Pareto Optimally beneficial for all individuals, groups, organizations, and societies:

1. *All markets must be fully competitive*: Each productive company is located between two markets: one for the output goods and services sold by that company and one for the input workers, materials, and monies purchased by that company. Both of these markets must be fully open and competitive for a company to be able to claim that they have reached a Pareto Optimal level of economic efficiency and thus are truly contributing to the well-being of customers, suppliers, and the overall society.

   The problem, of course, is that there are degrees of competition within all markets, both those for input labor, material, and capital and those for output goods and services. Companies pursue competitive advantage through product and process innovations, supplier and distributor relationships, scale and scope economies, government permits and supports, et cetera. Ideally, all of these advantages would be open to each of the competitors, and any advantage gap should be quickly closed by competitive reactions, but that frequently does not happen due to relative power positions in the markets.

   Relative power positions in the markets do not seem to have been an issue in the intercompany exchanges that took place between the participants in the horizontal joint venture markets of the deepwater drilling project or in the vertical value chain markets of the residential mortgages process. One could perhaps argue that these intercompany exchanges were a bit too price conscious (not enough room for physical and environmental safety considerations) in the market exchanges of the deepwater drilling industry, and a bit too price unconscious (more than enough room for financial product/service quality manipulations) in the market exchanges of the residential mortgage industry. In both instances, however, the prices were apparently set by multiple exchanges conducted over time between different managers apparently working for the best interests of their relative employers in markets with numerous alternative suppliers, and thus any complaints here have to be muted.

In many other instances, however, intracompany exchange markets are not fully open or truly competitive. Those types of exchanges will be described in two of the latter case examples in this book. In the first of these, the wealthy clients at the start of the value chain and the financial institutions at the end had such dominance that they could establish a lengthy series of highly complex but functionally unneeded exchanges to confuse federal tax authorities. These complex but unneeded exchanges were legal simply because they were so unneeded; no regulator or legislator had ever conceived that they might be a means of evasion. In the second example, the patent-holding firms at the start of the value chain and the large chain retailers at the end had such dominance that they could enforce severe price concessions upon the intermediate participants in order to raise their own profits. These severe price concessions were legal at the time because they took effect overseas. They did, however, result in such substantial cost-cutting responses at that overseas intermediate level in the value chain that they brought about major safety problems on preschool children's toys.

The question then becomes, "How open and competitive do markets have to be in order to be fully economically efficient and thus result in Pareto Optimal outcomes that impartially distribute the benefits of production between individuals, organizations, and societies?" That is a question that is impossible to answer with any precision, and therefore other evaluative principles, standards, or rules need to be considered. Those other evaluative principles, standards, or rules will be addressed in the latter chapters of this book.

2. *All participants must be fully informed*: Each productive company is located, not only directly between the output markets for goods and services and the input markets for workers, materials, and funds, but also indirectly between the individual consumers who buy the products they most want to possess and the individual suppliers who sell the resources they (the sellers) least want to retain. One assumption of the Pareto Optimal outcome of economically efficient decisions and actions is that the productive firms within each industry have fully informed the individual customers about the functions (what they are designed to do) and the characteristics (what are the limits on that performance) of the output products or services they are offering for sale. Another assumption is that the individual suppliers in each industry have also

fully informed the productive firms about the functions (what they are capable of doing) and characteristics (what are the limits on that performance) of the resources they are offering for sale. In short, to reach true economic efficiency in market exchanges, it must be "buyers be informed" rather than "buyers beware."

In the exchanges between the many participants in the horizontal joint venture of the deepwater drilling industry, it would appear that all buyers had been adequately informed. Certainly there was no evidence that any information had been deliberately withheld. For example, everyone on both side of this market transaction understood that a blowout preventer with a single shutoff shear had a three out of a hundred probability of failure, but one joint venture participant went ahead and sold it and another joint venture participant went ahead and bought it. It is always improper to infer motives, but one could guess that the decision was logically based upon an expected risk/reward calculation where—unfortunately, due to the newness of the deepwater drilling endeavor—the risk could not be accurately computed and massive damage did result.

In the exchanges between the many participants in the vertical value chain of the residential mortgage industry, however, misinformation can only be described as deliberately endemic and thoroughly widespread. Home owners gave erroneous information about occupation types, income levels, and credit ratings to the mortgage brokers; mortgage brokers passed along that erroneous data to the multiservice banks and investment firms who first created the residential mortgage based securities and the CDO, and then sent those RMBS and CDO instruments to the rating agencies for their approval, and finally sold these approved instruments to individual and institutional investors without—at any of those steps—mentioning the underlying lies and evasions.

In this instance, the amount and extent of buyer misinformation throughout the vertical value chain of the residential mortgage industry eventually destroyed that industry, but in less egregious examples, the question becomes, once again, what is the limit? How much consumer/purchaser information is needed? That is a question, similar to how much competition is required, that is impossible to answer with any precision, and therefore other evaluative principles, standards, or rules need to be considered. Those other evaluative principles, standards, or rules will, once again, be addressed in chapters 4 and 5 of this book.

3. *All external costs must be fully included*: External costs are the expenses imposed upon others without their consent; they are termed "external" because they are outside the market transactions. They include injuries in the workplace, damages to the environment, harms to the society, wrongs to the economy, interferences with the government, et cetera. Theoretically companies should (a) recognize each external cost they are imposing upon other individuals, groups, organizations, or even societies without their consent; (b) estimate the total amount of that cost they are imposing by multiplying the statistical probability of the occurrence times the financial value of the impact; (c) divide the total amount of that cost by the number of output units (goods or services) whose production and sale will create this external cost; and (d) add that cost per output unit to the sale price of the product or service.

This complex four-step process allegedly will: (a) ensure that all external costs to be imposed upon others without their consent will be reflected in the market prices for those goods and services; (b) thus limit the sales of those goods or services to those individuals, groups, or organizations that need them so badly that they are willing to pay the extra cost; and (c) ensure that the producing firm that imposed these external costs upon others without their consent will have the cash reserves to pay the judgment, fine, or assessment when that complete external cost is finally determined and those affected finally compensated.

The multiple companies cooperating in the horizontal joint venture of the deepwater drilling industry may have had competitive markets and informed customers/suppliers in each intercompany exchange, but each of them totally neglected the economic efficiency assumption of external costs. All eight of the so-called troubling questions described in chapter 1: (a) dealt with managerial decisions and actions, either on board the Deepwater Horizon or at the district offices of the involved firms on shore; (b) substantially decreased the cost of the drilling operation but incrementally increased the probability of a disastrous blowout, explosion, and fire: and thus (c) imposed substantial external costs upon very large sections of the general population within the Gulf region without their consent.

The problem here, as was also expressed in chapter 1, comes in computing the statistical probability and the financial impact, of a blowout, explosion, and fire that—when it did eventually occur—killed 11 employees, injured many others, severely damaged the Gulf environment, ruined for a time the sea-food gathering and processing industries dependent upon that environment, and interfered with the lives and livelihoods of literally hundreds of thousands of permanent residents, business owners, and summer vacationers along the Gulf coast. Again, we believe that it is necessary to consider other evaluative principles, standards, or rules, not to get a different estimate of the costs because that is so difficult if not totally impossible but to look at the matter from totally different perspectives of those outcomes.

Conclusions from Chapter 3

What are the conclusions of chapter 3? Economic efficiency provides a very decent first step in evaluating managerial decisions and actions that benefit some individuals, groups, organizations, and even societies while harming others, or that recognize the rights of some of those same individuals, groups, organizations, and societies, while ignoring the right of others. It provides this very decent first step because: (a) the outcome of economic efficiency has the potential to become the common good—the maximum output of the most-wanted goods and services for the full society at the minimum input of the least wanted monetary, material, and skill resources of the full society—and (b) the input and output markets have the potential to provide impartial mechanisms for the distribution of those benefits and the allocation of those harms that are all part of the common good among the individual suppliers and the individual consumers that form the full society.

But, due to the difficulty of adjusting in meaningful ways to the underlying assumptions that: (a) all input resource markets and all out-product markets are fully competitive; (b) all input resource buyers and output product customers are fully informed; and (c) all external costs imposed upon others without their consent have been fully recognized, estimated, and included in the product pricing, something more is needed. And, even further, something more is also needed to make up for *the total lack of any inclusion of the issue of the rights recognized versus right ignored in the economic efficiency construct.*

One candidate for that "something more" is legal conformity. Simply expressed this phrase means, "Always obey the law because the law ideally represents the combined standards of individual, group, and organizational conduct held by a majority of the population." The positives and the problems of this simple sounding but complex performing dictum will be addressed in chapter 4.

CHAPTER 4

Applying the Evaluative Construct of Legal Conformity

Foreign tax havens tend to be small independent states with stable governments, low taxes, strict privacy rules, good communication and transportation facilities, and discrete legal and financial services. They often are located in pleasant tourist destinations such as the Caribbean islands (Antigua, Bahamas, Barbados, Bermuda, et cetera) or the Alpine regions of Europe (Switzerland and Liechtenstein) that citizens from economically advanced countries could quietly visit and confidentially make arrangements for the transfer of substantial sums of money that would then be immune from all of the income, investment, and inheritance taxes of their home countries.

For years, the actual amounts of those "sizeable sums" of money that had either been entrusted to discrete local bankers in the smaller tax havens or moved to equally discrete but more technically adept banking centers in the larger participating countries remained unknown. There were estimates in the hundreds of billions of dollars, but the secrecy stayed firmly intact and there was no exact knowledge of the amounts or the owners. Then, in February, 2008, a former employee of the LTG Bank in Liechtenstein—a small principality located in the Alps between Switzerland and Austria with just 37,000 residents—evidently felt that he had been inappropriately discharged, and proceeded to provide tax authorities around the world with the financial records he had copied of 1,400 persons who had opened accounts and deposited funds at that bank. The names of 100 US citizens were on that list.[1]

LTG Bank has long held a reputation as one of the major tax-haven banks. It is owned by members of the ruling family in Liechtenstein, and consequently was strongly protected by the laws of that country. Those laws provided no protection, however, to the US citizens whose names had been revealed, particularly given that the released records of some of them indicated that they also had secretive accounts at the United Bank of Switzerland (UBS). A senior official in the private banking division of UBS, Bradley Birkenfeld, happened to be traveling in Florida at this time, visiting some of these dual clients who had been identified. Mr. Birkenfeld was arrested as he approached the residence of one of those clients; his computer and other records confiscated, and he was charged with conspiracy to defraud the IRS.[2]

Some of the records seized when Mr. Birkenfeld was arrested seemed to indicate that the private banking division of UBS had thousands of US clients who held billions of dollars of assets in what the bank termed "undeclared accounts," meaning that neither the person owning the account nor the bank holding the account had notified the IRS of the existence of the account. Both of those actions were required by US law. Consequently, the US Justice Department, at the request of the IRS, filed an administrative summons against UBS demanding that this bank release the names of all US citizens who owned undeclared and therefore untaxed accounts held by UBS in Switzerland, and reveal the holdings in those accounts. Both of those actions were prohibited under long-standing Swiss law.[3]

Switzerland is a smallish country, with a population of just 7.7 million people, sited in the scenic Alpine region of Central Europe between France, Germany, and Italy. Despite its location between historically contentious neighbors, it has a carefully maintained long history of neutrality; the last war in which it was actively engaged took place in 1815. It is a mountainous country so there is limited large-scale agriculture. It is a landlocked nation so there is little global commerce. It lacks the basic resources of coal and ore so that there is almost no heavy industry. But, it is one of the most prosperous nations on earth, with a 2005 GDP, converted to US dollars, of $67,000 per person. That prosperity is based upon luxury resorts, high-quality textiles, the precision production of watches and scientific/medical instruments, and the ready availability of private banks.

For years, these private banks were small, family owned, and exceedingly discrete. During the 1800s, it became a criminal offense in Switzerland for bankers to reveal either the names or the holdings of their clients, and this lawful privacy brought the deposits of many wealthy families throughout Europe as frequent wars racked that region. Following World War II, however, the family-owned banks began to coalesce into publicly held institutions. By 2000, the two premier ones, Credit Suisse and UBS, were equal in size to those in New York or London, and engaged in many of the same commercial banking and investment banking practices. The wealth management divisions of those large banks, and of the many smaller ones that remained active throughout Switzerland, however, maintained the traditional Swiss practices of extreme discretion and absolute privacy for their clients.

It is important at this point to understand that the US distinction between tax avoidance (purchasing municipal bonds whose interest payments are tax free, or investing for capital gains which are charged a far lower rate than dividend payments) and tax evasion (failing to report income actually received) is not as clear in Europe as in the United States. Part of the reason is that many European families, and not just those who are exceedingly wealthy, have survived based upon their undisclosed incomes during the many wars and recessions that have plagued that continent. A more important part of the reason, however, is that income taxes play a far less important role in financing governmental services in Europe than in the United States.

Most of the tax revenues collected by European nations (Great Britain is the major exception) come from "value added" taxes added to the retail prices of all consumer goods and services sold within each country. These taxes consist of small percentages assessed at each of the sequential stages in the production and distribution of those goods and services. They are based upon the difference between the direct cost of the material and labor expended at each stage, and the transfer price to the next stage. They are easily computed, permanently recorded in the audited accounts of each company, reliably remitted to the government in each country by those companies, but actually paid, of course, by the final purchaser of the goods and services: the retail customer. It is still believed to be a reasonably equitable tax because the final value added to the price is much higher for luxury goods than for daily necessities.

The tax systems of the United States and Europe are clearly different, and the banking practices in Switzerland that were adjusted to those differences have created conflicts with the United States. These conflicts primarily concern the non-payment of US taxes by some US citizens. The Senate Permanent Subcommittee on Investigations (SPSI) has estimated that the US government loses $100 billion per year in tax revenues due to offshore tax abuses.[4] There have since been numerous negotiated attempts to reduce that annual loss, all of which are explained in some detail in that SPSI report.

Switzerland first entered into a tax treaty with the United States in 1951. Under that treaty, Switzerland agreed to exchange information in criminal cases involving tax fraud, which had been defined as situations in which a taxpayer used, or intended to use, forged or falsified documents. This had originally been deemed as a satisfactory proposal by the IRS, but the US Justice Department quickly found that it was necessary to produce the forged or falsified documents in Swiss courts in order to prevail, and those were generally difficult to find and truly relevant in only a few of the major tax-evasion cases. Consequently, the United States in 2000 adopted a new initiative called the Qualified Intermediary (QI) program, which was signed *not* by the countries that wished to trade with the United States but by the "intermediaries" or banks that wanted to interact with financial institutions within the United States.[5]

This QI agreement required those banks to report all US source income to the US government. US source income was defined as all income, whether in the form of dividends, interest, salary, bonus payments, or capital gains, that came from a source within the United States and was credited to an account owned by a citizen of the United States. Over 7,000 foreign financial institutions signed the QI agreement, including most of the major banks within Switzerland, and promised to participate actively in the program.

Compliance, however, has been low and participation stodgy. Some of the foreign banks that had agreed to participate in the program simply replaced the stocks and bonds of US-based corporations in accounts held by US citizens with stocks and bonds from non-US firms. Others changed the name of the account holder from that of the US citizen to the name of a newly set up foreign corporation owned by the US citizen. These foreign corporations frequently were created in a complex series of interrelated corporations, trusts, and foundations to hide the true beneficial ownership, as shown in the example below that had been arranged in 1997 in anticipation of the QI program. The final name is that of a US citizen:

> Beverly Park Corporation was incorporated in Delaware on January 3, 1997, by a registered Delaware agent, Corporation Trust Company. Beverly Park is wholly owned by Cordera Holdings Pty Ltd., which is

owned by Franley Holdings Pty Ltd, which is owned by LGF Holdings Pty Ltd, which is in turn owned by Frank Lowy Trust.[6]

United Bank of Switzerland followed the more direct practice of replacing all US stocks and bonds held by US citizens with equivalent investments in non-US firms for their existing private account clients, and insisting that all new clients sell their US holdings before opening a private account. Those policies were fully implemented by 2002, and in November of that year, a letter was sent to all US clients stating that UBS could not be forced to disclose a Swiss account held by a US citizen as long as that account contained no US securities, even if UBS knew that the account holder was a US taxpayer obligated under US tax law to report the account and its contents to the IRS. That letter continued that the reporting obligations applied to the account holder personally, not to UBS, and thus UBS had broken no US law or QI obligation and so could not be forced to divulge any information or be subject to any legal claim.[7]

Six years later, however, on February 18, 2009, the United Bank of Switzerland reached what was termed a "deferred prosecution agreement" with the US government to: (a) pay a $780 million fine for conspiring to defraud the IRS by failing to report the annual incomes of secretive accounts held by US citizens; and (b) to confirm the names of 270 US citizens who were believed to hold some of those accounts through their ownership of intentionally constructed foreign corporations, trusts, and foundations. A deferred prosecution agreement is not a dismissal of the charges; instead, it is a formal contract not to bring those charges to trial unless the accused person or organization fails to complete the full terms of the contract.[8]

In quick succession, on February 19, 2009, the US Justice Department filed a new claim seeking to force UBS to release the names of all US citizens who held unreported accounts in the private wealth management division of that bank. It was estimated that 52,000 US citizens held such accounts. These two actions were major changes in the ongoing battle between Swiss banks and the US government.[9]

What happened? What forced the United Bank of Switzerland to move, in just over six years, from an assurance to its account holders that UBS had broken no US laws or QI obligations and thus could never be forced to divulge any information or ever be subject to any claim, to a formal agreement to pay a huge fine, to identify a small group of holders despite the elaborate disguises that had been erected, and perhaps eventually be forced to reveal the names of all US holders of private accounts within that bank?

It was soon disclosed that bankers in the private wealth management division of UBS had not waited in Switzerland for US clients to come to them, or to be referred to them from smaller banks in other tax havens, or to be sent to them by some of the many attorneys, consultants, and advisors who worked on tax matters throughout the world. Instead, many of the UBS private bankers working in Switzerland had gone to the United States looking for clients,[10] apparently in violation of strict UBS guidelines.

The UBS had issued, in 2004, a policy statement that placed very explicit restrictions on the activities of their Swiss-based bankers if they traveled to the United States:

> UBS will not advertise and market for its services with material going beyond generic information relating to the image of UBS AG and its brand in the U.S.
>
> UBS AG may not establish relationships for securities products or services with new clients resident in the U.S. with the use of U.S. jurisdictional means.
>
> UBS should ensure that:
>
> - No marketing or advertising activity targeted to U.S. persons takes place in the United States.
> - No solicitation of account opening takes place in the United States.
> - No cold calling or prospecting into the United States takes place.
> - No negotiation or conclusion of contracts takes place within the United States.
> - No carrying or transmitting of cash or other valuables out of the United States takes place.
> - No routine certification of signatures, transmission of completed account documentation, or related administrative activity on behalf of UBS AG takes place.
> - Employees do not carry on substantial activities at fixed locations while in the United States thereby establishing an office or maintaining a place of business.[11]

Mr. Birkenfeld, the UBS banker from Switzerland, who had been arrested while visiting a UBS client in Florida (one of those who had been identified

through the unauthorized distribution of Bank of Liechtenstein documents by a dissatisfied prior employee of that bank) subsequently agreed
to become a US government witness to avoid criminal prosecution. He
explained at the hearing of the Senate Subcommittee on Investigations
that he had been unaware of these restrictions until a colleague showed
him a copy of the 2004 policy statement. He added that the policies
described in that statement entirely contradicted the activities that were
detailed in his formal job description.

Mr. Birkenfeld went on to say that essentially his job, while on assigned
visits to the United States, was to find new clients:

> You might go to sporting events. You might go to car shows, wine tast-
> ings. You might deal with real estate agents. You might deal with attor-
> neys. It's really where the rich people hang out; go and talk to them.
> It wasn't difficult to walk into a party with a business card, and then
> someone asks you, "What do you do?" and you say, Well, I work for a
> bank in Switzerland and we manage money there and open accounts.
> And people immediately would recognize, "Oh, this is someone who
> could open new business by opening accounts."[12]

Travel to the United States by UBS bankers based in Switzerland not only
was allowed by UBS; it was encouraged. From 2003 to 2008, roughly
20 UBS bankers made over 300 trips to the United States; many of these
bankers designated the purpose of their trips on the US Custom Service
port-of-entry forms as leisure. There was some truth to those claims. They
attended many of the major professional golf matches, tennis tournaments,
and sailing regattas. Doubtless those were pleasant events, but the job
performance of the visiting Swiss bankers was measured, and rewarded,
by the "net new money" (NNM) raised from the contacts each of them
established during their trips.[13]

> One client could make your numbers, or 10 to 25 could make your
> numbers. It's very hard to gauge that. And again, when people aren't
> paying tax in the three areas I told you—inheritance, income and capi-
> tal gains—it's quite easy for people to bring money to you. They're very
> interested to bring as much money to the bank as possible.[14]

These accounts that were designed to "bring as much money to the bank
as possible" to avoid paying US taxes in the three basic areas of inheritance,
income, and investment gains were actually opened during subsequent

visits by the client and members of his or her family to Switzerland. This was done to maintain the primacy of Swiss law. During that visit, methods for transferring funds through a series of apparently foreign-owned companies, foundations, and trusts were arranged for each client, as were also the means for reporting on the performance of those funds after they had been received and invested. All reporting was done verbally, during US client visits to Switzerland or Swiss banker visits to the United States, to avoid leaving written records. Income from the undisclosed and hidden investments was returned, when verbally requested, to the client and members of his or her family through the same series of apparently foreign-owned companies, foundations, and trusts that had been set up for the original funds transfer.

During trips to the United States to make those verbal reports on performance or to receive verbal requests for payment, the Swiss-based private bankers used code names for the clients, encrypted information for the reports, prepaid cell phones for contacts, and frequent changes of hotels, restaurants, and rental cars for anonymity. In short, this was a deliberately secretive but professionally run operation. No one carried suitcases of cash about, although Mr. Birkenfeld admitted that at one time he had brought a small fortune in diamonds to a client in the United States. He got them through the US customs hidden in a tube of toothpaste.[15]

Had the disgruntled former employee of LTG Bank in Liechtenstein not widely distributed copies of the client account documents he illegally took from that bank, and had some of those illegally obtained documents not concerned US clients, and had Bradley Birkenfeld from UBS not been found actually visiting one of those clients within the United States, all of the current information about undeclared accounts of US taxpayers held by UBS Bank would have remained hidden and confidential. But all that did happen, and some, but not all, of that information has now been revealed. The question we want to address in the balance of this chapter is: "Does the commonly stated prescription 'Always obey the law' apply in this situation?" After all, there are two separate and vastly different laws.

Before moving on to that question, however, we want to make clear that the concealment of the taxable income of US citizens from the tax-enforcement authorities of the US government is not the exclusive province of Swiss banks. Numerous American law firms and accounting firms have been similarly accused, though here the usual method of concealment was to devise complex financial transactions rather than to open foreign bank accounts. KPMG, one of the "big four" accounting firms, provided the most infamous example. This "infamous example" of income concealment was made possible though a complex series of financial transactions that essentially made large income amounts disappear has been described in understandable detail in a report titled *U.S. Tax Shelter Industry: The Role of Accountants, Lawyers and Financial Professionals* that was prepared by the Senate Committee on Homeland Security and Governmental Affairs (SCHS&GA) and issued on November 28, 2003.[16]

KPMG, following a lengthy dispute with the IRS over the use of what was termed a Bond Lined Issue Premium Structure (BLIPS) tax-evasion method, agreed in August, 2005, as part of a deferred prosecution agreement to: (a) pay imposed penalties of $456 million without benefit of offsetting liability insurance proceeds or income tax reductions; (b) accept a monitor to supervise an agree-upon program of governance restructuring and organizational change; (c) severely limit future income tax service offerings; and (d) provide no legal assistance or monetary payments in lieu of that assistance to the senior partners and professional employees who were expected to later be charged personally in the case.[17]

> In the statement of facts [that accompanied the settlement], KPMG acknowledges that the firm's partners "assisted high-net-worth United States citizens to evade United States individual income taxes on billions of dollars in capital gain and ordinary income by developing, promoting and implementing unregistered and fraudulent tax shelters.[18]

The high-net-worth US citizens who made use of the BLIPS transactions were required to have a capital gain, bonus award, or retirement benefit of at least $20 million during a single calendar year. Those well-paid citizens did not have to go to KPMG. Instead, KPMG came to them as part of an aggressive marketing campaign directed by senior partners within the firm, including the deputy chairman, vice chairman, and head of the Tax Department. It was believed that this BLIPS tax shelter, during the short time it had been in use, had created more than $11 billion in artificial losses and had enabled about 600 US citizens to avoid paying some $2.5 billion in US taxes.[19]

The BLIPS tax shelter was able to record a $20 million or more loss even though the well-paid citizens who had a $20 million or more gain for a given year were able to retain all of that $20 million or more except for the commission that had to be paid to KPMG. There were also no associated reductions in any of that person's other assets. How can an investor report a loss of $20 million or more in cash and yet retain exactly the same personal net worth? By a series of successive steps that Senator Carl Levin, the chair of the Senate Committee that investigated this practice, claimed were so "convoluted and complex... [that they were] MEGOs—that means my eyes glaze over."[20]

The sequence of steps described below is taken from the report titled *U.S. Tax Shelter Industry* that was prepared by the US Senate Committee on Homeland Security and Governmental Affairs in 2003. It does, however, leave out some of the more "convoluted and complex" of these steps that appear to have been designed more to confuse the regulators than to forward the procedures so that we will be able to focus on the ones that actually accomplished the stated objective of recording a $20 million loss without—a seemingly impossible task under the time-tested rules of double-entry accounting—changing the recorded net worth of the individual involved. Now, on to these steps that in KPMG parlance were termed simple and innocent-sounding "tax planning."[21]

1. KPMG established a limited liability company (LLC) in the name of their new tax-planning client.

2. KPMG then introduced that client to an investment banking firm that had agreed to provide financing for all of KPMG's tax shelter LLCs, and to a private investment counselor who had agreed to manage the tax shelter funds for all of those tax shelter LLCs.

3. The client then made an equity investment of $1.4 million in his or her new tax shelter LLC. This amount was always 7 percent of the amount that the client wished to protect. 7 percent of $20 million is obviously $1.4 million.

4. The investment banking firm that had been introduced to the client by KPMG then provided the client's LLC with a seven-year term loan of $50 million—two and a half times the amount that was to be tax protected—at a high rate of interest: 16 percent per year. Next, the investment bank provided the client's LLC with a $20 million premium—the amount that was to be tax protected—allegedly to reward that client's willingness to pay such a high rate of interest. This premium was said to be an incentive for the client to maintain the full amount of the high-interest loan over the seven years, which would have provided the investment bank with total interest payments of $56 million. The premium did not have to be repaid except given one

voluntary and unexpected action on the part of the client: a request that the entire program be cancelled. As such, the premium could not be listed as a liability on the LLC's balance sheet. Instead, it had to be listed as semi-equity.

5. The client's LLC now had a cash balance of $71.4 million that was composed of $1.4 million equity, $20 million semi-equity, and $50 million high-interest debt. The private investment counselor who had been recommended by KPMG and approved by the investment bank now took over active management of that cash balance, under the policy guidance of the investment bank.

6. The private investment counselor began to invest the capital at his or her disposal in foreign currency trading. Foreign currency trading can be quite profitable for knowledgeable advisors, but that form of speculation can also be almost guaranteed to eventually result in at least one substantial loss. When that loss occurred, the client, it was alleged but not proven, had been told by KPMG to panic, to fire the investment counselor, and to close the LLC that held $71,400,000 plus or minus the remaining balance from the foreign exchange trading activities.

7. When the KPMG client closed his or her LLC the $50 million loan went back to the investment bank together with the $20 million premium. That premium had been awarded to the client to atone for the 16 percent interest rate that was to be charged on the loan, and once the full loan amount had been returned that premium was no longer deserved and, as part of the original agreement, had to be returned.

8. The investment bank received full repayment of the loan and of the premium plus the 16 percent annual interest on the loan that had been paid for the number of months the LLC existed, and was thus made whole. The private investment counselor received his or her salary for the number of months the LLC existed, and was thus made whole. The client recovered most of his or her original $1.4 million investment in the LLC, less the loan interest payments, investor counselor wages, and the exchange trading loss (that usually was more than covered by the earlier exchange trading profits), and so he or she was made reasonably whole, *but with a $20 million recorded loss in owner's equity.*

What do these two tax-saving plans from UBS and KPMG mean for our question as to whether the simple dictum "Always conform to the law" is a adequate guide for managers to follow in making decisions or taking actions that may benefit some individuals, groups, or organizations while harming others, or that recognize the rights of some individuals, groups, or organizations while ignoring the rights of others?

Interpretations of the applicable laws are clearly central in both situations. To answer the "Is legal conformity an adequate guide for managers to follow in making decisions and taking actions that have the potential to impact, in both positive and negative ways, the well-being and rights of other individuals, groups, and organizations?" question, we have to deal with the interpretation and the application of those laws, and that requires starting at the beginning. We thus propose to look at: (a) definition of the law; (b) formation of the law; (c) imperfections in the law; (d) commercialization of the law; (e) the concept of competitive justice in law; (f) evaluative standards for the outcome of law; (g) evaluative standards for the process of law; (h) what all this means to the practice of law; and (i) our conclusion to the chapter. That's a full plate. Let's get started.

Definition of the Law

Law can be defined as a set of rules that prescribe the ways in which individuals, groups, and organizations should act in their relationships with other individuals, groups, and organizations within a given society. Laws are requirements to act in that way, not just expectations or suggestions or recommendations to act following those provisions. There is an aura of insistency about the law; it defines what you *must* do to be considered a lawful and respected member of your society.

These requirements to act, or more generally requirements *not to act* in a given way—many if not most of our laws are negative regulations, telling us what we should not do in certain situations—have a set of characteristics that separate our societal laws from our cultural norms. There are five of these characteristics that are considered to be essential for a given set of rules to be viewed as valid requirements for the members of a certain society:

1. *Uniform*: The requirements to act or not to act have to be uniform in conception to be considered part of the law. That is, they must be limited to individuals, groups, or organizations with certain characteristics facing situations with specific conditions. If two requirements to act or not to act contradict each other, neither can be termed a law because obviously people cannot simultaneously obey both.

2. *Universal*: The requirements to act or not to act also have to be universal in application to be considered part of the law. That is, they must

apply equally to all individuals, groups, or organizations with similar characteristics facing parallel circumstances. People tend not to obey laws that they believe apply only to themselves, and not to others.

3. *Accessible*: The requirements to act or not to act have to be published, in written form, so that the rules are available to everyone within the society to be considered part of the law. Everyone may not have the time to read or the training to understand those rules, which tend to be complex due to the need to uniformly define what constitute similar characteristics and parallel circumstances. However, trained professionals—attorneys—are available to interpret and explain the law, so that ignorance of the published rules is not considered to be a valid excuse.

4. *Accepted*: The requirements to act or not to act in a given way have to be generally obeyed. If most members of the society do not voluntarily obey the law, too great a burden will be placed on the last provision, that of enforcement.

5. *Enforced*: The requirements to act or not to act in a given way have to be enforced. Members of society have to understand that they will be compelled to obey the law if they do not choose to do so voluntarily. People have to recognize that if they disobey the law, and if that disobedience is noted and can be proven to have occurred, they will suffer some loss of convenience, time, money, freedom, or life. There is, as was earlier noted, an aura of insistency about the law. There is also, or ideally should be, an aura of inevitability; law basically defines what will happen if you don't follow the uniform, universal, published, and accepted set of societal rules.

The intent of this chapter is to examine not so much the characteristics of the law as the sources of its legitimacy. Why should we obey the law? Is the reason solely that we fear the negative consequences of disobedience—the potential loss of some portion of our convenience, time, money, freedom, or life—or is there a positive acceptance of the law among large numbers of people, and does that positive acceptance come from a sense of participating in the methods of formation or agreeing with the goals of application? The next section looks at the process of formation.

Formation of the Law

It is possible to make the argument that within a participative democracy there is a positive acceptance of the law by many if not most of the citizens, that the law under such a governmental process reflects to a very considerable extent the personal standards of conduct of a majority of the population. Personal standards of conduct, as were described in chapter 2, are our intuitive evaluations of what we judge to be legitimate individual, group, and organizational behavior. They are the subjective means we all use to decide whether our actions, and those of the other individuals, groups, and organizations with whom we live and work and associate, are those that we believe to be—once again, using those logically imprecise though individually meaningful terms—right or wrong, fair or unfair, just or unjust.

Let us explain once more that while all of us use those terms of right or wrong, fair or unfair, just or unjust, we should all also agree that they mean different things to different people. Those words, seemingly so simple, have proven over millennia, not just centuries, to be impossible to define in terms that would be agreeable to everyone. But we all have an intuitive understanding of behavior that is acceptable—and sometimes even inspirational—to us as individuals. Those are the rules that most of us as citizens choose to follow, and the rules we believe that other citizens should either choose to follow or be compelled to follow. That is, those rules are our understanding of what the law should be. All too frequently, however, it is not.

Personal standards of behavior differ between people because the goals, norms, beliefs, and values upon which they depend also differ, and those goals, norms, beliefs, and values in turn differ because of variations in the religious and cultural traditions and in the economic and social situations in which each of the citizens within a participatory democracy are inherently immersed. These relationships were earlier depicted in a diagram in chapter 2, and that diagram is reproduced (see figure 4.1) to remind readers of what we have in mind.

How do these personal standards of conduct, differing between people and at least partially dependent upon the extraneous factors of religious and cultural traditions and economic and social situations that also differ between people, become law? Individuals tend to associate with other individuals who have closely similar goals, norms, beliefs, and values and gradually they collect in small groups. Those small groups tend to interact with other small groups that have roughly similar goals, norms, beliefs, and values and slowly they coalesce into formal organizations. These formal organizations tend to focus upon the most widely supported goals, norms, beliefs, and values of their members, and over time build the numbers, the funds, and the contacts needed to influence the

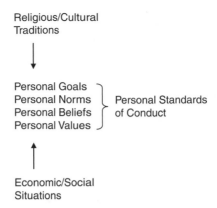

Figure 4.1 Causes of variations in the personal standards of conduct.

political processes that form the law. This sequence is also depicted in figure 4.2.

The problem with this overly simplified but reasonably accurate depiction of the process of the formation of law within a participatory democracy is that at each stage many compromises are required and many ideals left behind. Some of the goals, norms, beliefs, and values of individuals survive within the groups, but others are rejected. Some of the goals, norms, beliefs, and values of the groups become part of the stated objectives of an organization, but others are discarded. And finally, some of the organizations are able, through their size, money, knowledge, position, or power, to influence the formation of the law, but others fail in that endeavor. The outcome is a series of compromises that result not so much in integrated "big picture" programs to address evolving social concerns but much more often in packages of loosely connected and generally self-centered policies that intermix social concerns and organizational benefits. It is a process of national governance that has drawn adverse comments by a number of political leaders over the years. Two, in our view, are particularly memorable though their authors differ considerably in their degree of authentic democratic experience:

> "Democracy is the worst form of government except for all those other forms that have been tried from time to time" (Sir Winston Churchill, Prime Minister of Great Britain from 1940 to 1945 and from 1951 to 1955).[22]

> "Laws are like sausages; it is better not to see them being made" (Count Otto von Bismarck, Chancellor of the German Empire from 1870 to 1890).[23]

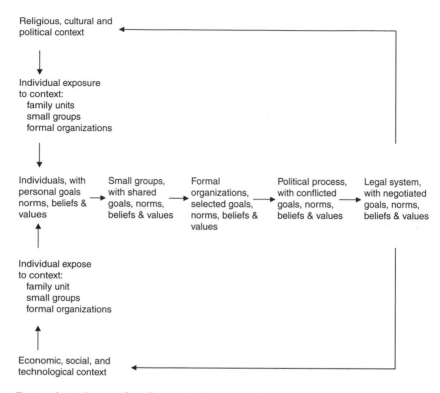

Figure 4.2   Causes of conflict in the formation of law.

Let us do more than accept the judgment of Sir Winston Churchill that participative democracy is the worst of all governmental forms except for all of the others. Let us acknowledge that there do exist multiple problems and obvious inefficiencies within this governmental structure, but still agree that it is by far the best among all of those others, and further admit that those of us who live and work and study within participative democracies are indeed fortunate persons. Our voices are frequently heard, and our votes almost always do count.

Imperfections of the Law

Human nature is such an unpredictable mixture of self-interested, organization-interested, and society-interested behaviors that we probably have to accept, along with our respect for the developmental history of law, that it will never be possible to fix all of the problems within our governmental structure or correct all of the imperfections in our resulting legal system, so perhaps we should endeavor to simply accept the former and gradually adjust to the latter. First, however, what exactly are those problems and imperfections?

1. *Compromised outcomes*: Individuals who hold personal goals, norms, beliefs, and values join groups that have shared goals, norms, beliefs, and values, those groups then coalesce into organizations that have stated goals, norms, beliefs, and values, and those organizations then contend with other organizations over the goals, norms, beliefs, and values that each believes should be transcribed into the specific programs and policies of the law. These programs and policies are the result of negotiated compromises. Each compromise is not quite as crude as "you accept our position on this one issue and we'll accept yours on this other," but overall they often either come very close to that decision point or totally block each other out. Explicit personal, group, and organizational self-interests do more than just sneak in. They are openly traded in a power-based process. And that means that—except in rare instances—the natural coherence of new programs to address evolving problems begins to fall apart. Laws simply are not as dedicated as they should be.

2. *Contextual advantages*: Demands for changes in the law come most often from the rapidly evolving economic, social, and technological contexts of society; resistance to those changes frequently comes from the far more stable cultural and religious contexts. This statement is not intended to be in any way a depreciation of those cultural and religious contexts. Stability is as important in human lives as is change. But, this distinction creates conflicts throughout the individual, group, and organizational stages of the formation of law. And, it has to be admitted that organizations that have a base in the economic, social, and technological sectors of society may not have more members than those in the cultural and religious areas, but they almost inevitably do have more money and position, and thus more influence or "clout" in the political process at the end, where it counts. Laws simply are not as balanced as they should be.

3. *Limited horizons*: Organizations based in the economic, social, and technological sectors of our society are far more subject to the problems brought about by rapidly occurring changes in their operating environments than are those based in the cultural and religious sectors,

and hence far more likely to respond to those ongoing changes with short-term, "fix-it-now and get it done" proposals for modifications or additions to the law. These are also the organizations that have the dominant positions in the political processes for the formation of the law, and this can lead to problems. Let us give a brief example here. During the 1980s, to increase the export trade of US manufacturers, clearly desirable to maintain jobs and balance deficits, it was proposed that the profits from the sales of exported goods be taxed at normal rates only when the profits from those sales were returned to the United States. No one thought that those corporate profits could be kept abroad, totally eliminate applicable US taxes, and used to build facilities or purchase competitors overseas, which would further reduce both US jobs and US taxes. Laws simply are not as foresighted as they should be.

4. *Neglected restrictions*: Specific problems arise in specific sectors within our society, and many of these problems, given the growing competition of global industries and the increasing importance of financial over human and material resources, occur in the economic sectors. Let us use the same example of special tax provisions for the export sales of US-manufactured goods. At the time those special provisions were proposed, US manufacturers were in trouble, and needed some help to meet competition from low-wage competitors based overseas. No one thought, however, that the same laws designed for product manufacturers could be applied to service providers, or even to corporate headquarters. Many of both have been moved overseas, which further reduced US jobs and US taxes. Laws simply are not as focused as they should be.

What has been the result of these compromised outcomes, contextual advantages, limited horizons, and neglected restrictions that appear to characterize the legal formation process? One result has been what we believe can legitimately be termed the "commercialization of law."

Commercialization of Law

The conclusion of the prior section on the formation of law was that many, perhaps even most, of our current laws have compromised outcomes, contextual advantages, limited horizons, and neglected restrictions. As a result there are gaps between laws, omissions within laws, and obsolete portions of laws. These imperfections create opportunities for law firms to work jointly with corporate clients in the design of new high-revenue services and innovative low-cost methods that may harm the well-being and ignore the rights of other individuals, groups, or organizations but fit neatly within the inexact boundaries of the existing laws.

We term these cooperative endeavors "commercialization of law," because law firms frequently search energetically at the request of certain clients to find relevant gaps, omissions, and obsolescent portions within the law, and then work cooperatively with those same corporate clients to develop new services and methods that are then marketed to other clients in addition to the original ones. Let us give a few brief but telling examples.

Arbitration is a form of alternative dispute resolution that many view as much more prompt and far less expensive than formal court proceedings. An allegedly neutral but professionally competent arbitrator listens as each side presents their view of the central issues, their understanding of the applicable laws, and their evidence of the supporting facts, and then provides an enforceable decision.

Because it is an enforceable decision, both sides have to agree to participate, but frequently that agreement is part of an underlying contract that one side—typically the customer in a company/customer service dispute—received and signed at the time the service started, but never fully understood or even read the contract. That is true of credit cards. When a dispute arises over charges on the card or payments to the card, the cardholder will find that he/she is required to submit to binding arbitration and forbidden to appeal to the courts.

This requirement to submit to arbitration probably would work well if the arbitrator who conducted the hearing and issued the verdict was truly neutral and impartial. But, how can "neutrality" and "impartiality" be defined and measured? Here is an obvious imperfection in the law. Arbitrators are normally employed on a part-time basis by for-profit companies such as the National Arbitration Forum or non-profit groups such as the American Arbitration Association. The credit card firms contract with one of those companies or groups to assign and compensate the arbitrators, but it is alleged that those arbitrators understand that the credit card firms are the ones that are actually selecting and then paying them to resolve a given dispute.

The selected arbitrators are generally attorneys, many of whom are retired and looking for a bit more income. The *New York Times* in a report prepared by the Associated Press stated that most arbitrators earned about $400 per hour, though some were paid over $10,000 per day.[24] That same *New York Times* article said that in cases where the arbitrators had been assigned and paid by the National Arbitration Forum to settle disputes between business firms and individual creditors, the rulings favored the business firms 94 percent of the time.

Here is the second example of the commercialization of law.[25] On some occasions, the more aggressive law firms do not wait for a client to request help in finding an applicable and profitable gap, omission, or obsolescence in the law. Instead, they find it on their own, and then market it to potential clients. This happened in 2007. A major law firm located in what had once been one of the most heavily industrialized and prosperous cities in the northeastern United States found such an opportunity in the changing technology base and employment needs of the local area.

Many of the larger corporations within this manufacturing-based city had suffered from foreign competition and been forced to close. Their place was gradually but steadily being taken by growing entrepreneurial ventures that specialized in informational and medical technologies. Faculty members at two nationally respected universities generated the ideas. Established banks and wealthy families provided the capital. The problem came in finding scientists and engineers who were competent in these new fields.

The young graduates in science and engineering from the local colleges and universities certainly had that competence, but it appeared that most of them wanted to move to Route 128 west of Boston or to the Silicon Valley south of San Francisco where they thought the companies were more solidly established and the living would be much livelier. The older scientists and engineers from the now-closed manufacturing plants wanted the jobs, but their skills seemed totally out of phase with the needs. Many were taking courses to improve their capabilities, but this new training took time and their lack of experience in close team working and quick innovative thinking was said to remain a problem.

There were plenty of fully competent and energetic scientists and engineers who were employed in India in jobs that required that close team working and quick innovative thinking. Most were graduates of the very advanced Indian Institutes of Technology, and many wanted to come to the United States because of the higher salaries and greater opportunities. But, for those well-qualified candidates to work in the United States, a potential employer had to obtain a "PERM," a certificate issued by the Employment and Training Administration of the Department of Labor stating that there were no US workers able, willing, qualified, and available to fill the position at the prevailing wage in the area of intended employment. The PERM, once received, could then be sent to the Customs and Immigration Service which would issue an immigration permit, often termed a "green card."

The law firm looked at the methods proposed by the Employment and Training Administration that a potential employer should follow to establish that there were "no US workers able, willing, qualified, and available" to fill a given position, and found that they were quite simple to satisfy. They then put together a seminar that they offered to clients and potential clients on how *not* to find qualified, able, and available US workers. Their advice was to advertise in newspapers young technically trained people tended not to read, go to job fairs that they tended not to attend, recruit at colleges where they normally did not enroll, and evaluate any resumes they did receive, despite these precautions, looking for defects in training, experience, or cooperative/innovative attitude.

The law firm videotaped their seminar and posted it on their web page as a form of advertising. A browser, perhaps alerted by one of the earlier attendees, found that videotape, edited it to capture the most inflammatory scenes and statements, and posted it on YouTube. It created an immediate and extensive firestorm of protest.

The four examples cited in this chapter—the UBS tax havens, the KPMG tax exclusions, the credit card arbitration requirements, and the law firm PERM instructions—all share four traits in common: (a) all were based upon an imperfection in the law; (b) all were heavily marketed, except for the credit card arbitration requirements which needed no marketing because they were already listed as a requirement in the original purchase contract; (c) each of these havens, exclusions, requirements, and instructions definitely harmed the well-being or abridged the rights of some other individuals, groups, organizations, or even societies; and (d) all, in the professed opinions of those most involved, not only were legal but legitimate; that is, they "conformed to a recognized principle or to accepted rules and standards." The legitimizing principle in this case was a new theory of competitive justice in law.

The Theory of Competitive Justice in Law

This new theory of competitive justice in law has an uncanny resemblance to the Pareto Optimal belief that if responsible people—managers and attorneys—would look after the interests of the organizations that employed them—the productive business firms—with total dedication, then major benefits would follow for all other individuals, groups, and organizations within the society. Any adverse effects upon others would be constrained, it was believed, by the competitive actions of markets, the political generosity of citizens, and—this is the new element that had been added—the impartial decisions of judges, juries, and arbitrators.

Competitive justice is a theory of the law that, due to the total dedication to a single interest that is required, is frequently termed "zealous advocacy." The belief is that law firms should represent the interests of each client with zealous—which often turns out to mean "highly aggressive"—advocacy, and should be prepared to defend those interests in "us against them" procedures before impartial judges, juries, and arbitrators or—though this would have been a definite second choice—in front of moderators and regulators who allegedly would be focused upon public rights and well-being. Law, it was declared, is an adversarial process, and the outcome of competent attorneys zealously defending the interests of their two contending clients before: (a) impartial judges and juries in a courtroom; (b) before neutral arbitrators at a hearing; or (c) before public rights focused moderators at a meeting would come as close as possible to the legal ideal of just, fair, and proper outcomes as can be expected in our imperfect world.

This view that clients come first has become not only common but nearly dominant throughout the legal profession. Indeed, what "market forces" and "rational decision making" are to current economic theory, "adversarial procedures" and "zealous advocacy" are to modern legal practice. Both sets of ideas are widely accepted, vigorously defended, and, if challenged, likely to get the one doing the challenging labeled an uncomprehending outsider. But, there are challenges here, and many of these come from inside the legal profession.

One of those critical insiders concerned about the current "energetically serve the interests of the client, and thus indirectly those of the society" focus of the law is Deborah Rhode, a senior faculty member at the Stanford Law School, and author of *In the Interests of Justice: Reforming the Legal Profession*. Professor Rhode, as you will soon observe, writes with elegance and style. She believes that all too many lawyers "have lost their connection to the values of social justice that sent them to the law in the first place," and that most Americans view their system of justice as "unwieldy, unintelligible and unaffordable."[26]

The central premise of her book is that the interests of the full society have played too small a part in determining the conduct codes and professional duties of attorneys, most of which were written by lawyers for lawyers. The result is that "our current system overvalues lawyers' and clients' interests at the expense of the public's."[27] On the specific issue of zealous advocacy before impartial judges and juries as the means of achieving social justice, she cites the underlying problems of impaired access, unequal resources, varying capabilities, and differing limits on access to information:

> The underlying premise that accurate results will emerge from competitive partisan presentations before disinterested tribunals depends on factual assumptions that seldom hold in daily practice. Most legal representations never receive oversight from an impartial decision maker. Many disputes never reach the point of formal legal complaint and of those that do, 90% settle before trial. Moreover, even cases that end up in court seldom resemble the bar's idealized model of adversarial processes. That model presupposes adversaries with roughly equal incentives, resources, capabilities, and access to relevant information. But those conditions are more the exception than the rule in a society that tolerates vast disparities in wealth, high litigation costs, and grossly inadequate access to legal assistance. As a majority of surveyed judges agreed, a mismatch in attorney skills can distort outcomes; a mismatch in client resources compounds the problem. In law, as in life, the haves generally come out ahead.[28]

Deborah Rhode is not alone in her concerns about the commercialization of law and the resultant focus on helping wealthy institutional and individual clients achieve their goals, often at the expense of less favored members of society. Others include both normative (how lawyers should act) and descriptive (how lawyers do act) scholars. Mary Ann Glendon is clearly on the normative side. She is a senior faculty member at the Harvard Law School, and author of *A Nation Under Lawyers: How the Crisis in the Legal Profession Is Transforming American Society.*[29] She too writes with enviable grace:

> In two successive revisions of its rules of ethics, the American Bar Association has removed almost all language of moral suasion, abandoning the effort to hold up an image of what a good lawyer ought

to be in favor of a minimalist catalogue of things a [bad] lawyer must not do.[30]

Law was supposed to be a learned and liberal profession, an art as well as a proud craft. The practice of law was a means of gaining a livelihood, but was to be pursued in the spirit of public service.[31]

"About half the practice of a decent attorney", lawyer-statesman Elihu Root is supposed to have said, "consists of telling would-be clients that they are damned fools and should stop."[32]

Let us add, before moving on to the next section on the descriptive rather than the normative theories criticizing the commercialization of law, that Elihu Root truly qualified for Mary Ann Glendon's honorary title of "lawyer-statesman." He had served, at the time he made those noted comments, as Scretary of war under President Warren McKinley, as secretary of state under President Theodore Roosevelt, and as senator from the state of New York from 1909 to 1915. Now, on to some of the empirically based concerns about the commercialization of law.

The descriptive criticisms of this new theory of law come not from law schools but from sociology and political science departments. The goal here was to empirically understand how the law actually worked, not to normatively propose how the law ideally should work. This approach had earlier been summarized by Roscoe Pound, then dean of the Harvard Law School, as "law-in-action" rather than "law in books."[33]

These social and political science researchers provided support for Dean Pound's observations. They went into court rooms, board rooms, and arbitration hearings, hoping to close the gap between the formal study of law and what they saw as the very different practice of law. Their findings were that the legal system was viewed by the corporate users and their advisory attorneys not so much as a collection of eminently rational principles, each firmly neutral in application and equally open to all members of the community, but rather as a set of bargaining chips and procedural possibilities which could be "played." The notion of law as a winnable game came to dominate the findings of most of these social/political science researchers.

The leading investigators in this "winnable game" field of study, which became known as Law and Society, were both at the University of Wisconsin: Stewart Macauley and Marc Galantier. Prof. Galantier published the first breakthrough study: "Why the Haves Come Out

Ahead: Speculations on the Limits of Legal Change."[34] He divided the legal system participants into two categories: "one shotters" and "repeat players." His findings were that the repeat players had an immense advantage. Having engaged in this supposed game on a repetitive basis over a period of years they developed: (a) acknowledged competence among their in-house attorneys; (b) first-in-line access to most outside specialists (c) extensive knowledge of bargaining strengths/weaknesses of probable opponents; (d) a "they're the ones we should contact first" reputation among potential clients; and finally (e) a "they're good people for us to get to know" access to elected lawmakers.

In short, it was not only that the practice of law had been commercialized as if that practice was just another industry with products to sell, but that this industry came with the same competitive advantages of economies of scale, benefits of experience, and spheres of influence as did most of the manufacturing and service areas within our economy. It became difficult to compete against the big law corporations, for that is exactly what so many of the earlier law partnerships had over time become.

What is the result of our review of the commercialization of the law and its critics? Our opinion is that we as a society have been left with a situation in which the law, through the difficulties of formation, is not as dedicated, balanced, foresighted, or inclusive as it should be, and in which the law firms, through the revenue-seeking opportunities we have termed commercialization, are not as socially oriented or as responsibly involved as they were alleged to have been in the past. Managers of both for-profit and non-profit organizations are now able to employ law firms to search for the gaps, omissions, and obsolete portions in the law that permit actions that benefit those organizations and their attorneys but often harm other individuals, groups, or organizations within society. What, if anything, can be done? We need first to look at the possibility of an *evaluative standard for the outcome of law*.

Evaluative Standard for the Outcome of Law

The evaluative standard for the outcome of law clearly has to be justice. But, justice is an ideal, not a reality. We can think generally about the policies and practices that might bring us closer to that ideal, but we can't specify exactly the actions that would lead us directly to the reality.

In short, we can't—despite 24 centuries of trying—define justice. This thought is perhaps best expressed by the novelist William Gaddis; the opening line of his *A Frolic of His Own* reads "Justice? You get justice in the next world; in this world you have the law."[35]

Why can't we define justice as the essential outcome of law? For exactly the same reasons that we and our ancestors, over the millennia we have previously mentioned, have been unable to specify the differences between right versus wrong, fair versus unfair, or proper versus improper. All three constructs are simply too interwoven a set of outcomes, with too individualized a set of criteria. Those outcomes—let us repeat—are the distribution of benefits, the allocation of harms, the acknowledgement of rights and the imposition of wrongs. Those criteria—let us also repeat—are people's varying goals, norms, beliefs and values that result in their differing standards of personal conduct.

Let us agree that we have been unsuccessful in the past at identifying evaluative standards for the *outcome* of law. Perhaps we should begin to consider evaluative standards for the *process* of law.

Evaluative Standards for the Process of Law

Law is both an art and a science. It is both a profession and a business. Scholars in the Society and Law field of study have even claimed that it is both a necessity and a game. In our view, the important duality is that law is both a set of established procedures and a group of interrelated outcomes, and it may do more to advance the cause of justice, imprecise as that construct may be, to address the procedures rather than continue to rely upon the outcomes.

These procedures appear to be derived about half from the lengthy and, it has to be admitted, largely honorable traditions of the law, and about half from the extensive and, once again it must be admitted, largely unresolved imperfections in the law. The law, as was explained in an earlier section of this chapter, is formed in a series of stages by which the goals, norms, beliefs, and values of individuals (that jointly form the behavioral standards of those individuals) are first endorsed by informal groups, then supported by formal organizations, next argued over by political parties, and finally compromised by elected representatives into the imperfect set of majority enacted regulations that fall short of the *uniform, universal, accessible, accepted, and enforced rules and standards* needed to regulate the behavior of all individuals, groups, and organizations within society. This is the legal formation process that fully merits, as we also explained in that earlier section, Winston Churchill's wise observation that democracy is the worst possible form of government except for all of the others that have been tried from time to time. In short, our laws may not be ideal but they are the best that we have—or are likely to have—to work with.

Many law firms and their clients have chosen to work with these existing but imperfect laws by searching for the numerous gaps, omissions, and obsolete portions within the law as written, and then as adjudicated, to locate specific regulations or rulings that could be commercially advantageous to certain of their clients, and then to aggressively defend their opinion of the legality of that newly discovered and highly profitable usage before the allegedly impartial judges, juries, and arbitrators of the judicial system.

This "we'll search for omissions and defend our positions" approach is what we have termed the "commercialization of law." We do not intend that term to convey a depreciatory view. Large law firms—and they must be large with specialists in all aspects of the law to do this both effectively and efficiently—attempt to provide what their clients or customers most want, just as do other commercial enterprises. What those clients or customers most want—it can be claimed in this situation—is legal permission to make a decision or take an action that they believe will result in greater profits for themselves, with the justification of those profits coming from impartial market forces. What these large law firms attempt to do—it does appear, once again in this situation—is to provide that legal permission by locating the relevant gaps, omissions, and obsolete portions of enacted and/or adjudicated laws, with the justification of the usage of those discovered inaccuracies and/or omissions through established conflict resolution procedures between equal opposing parties before impartial legal deciders. This is a lengthy and convoluted sentence, but the conclusion is clear: economics and law are closely entwined.

There have been numerous complaints about this closely entwined approach that can be said to be an attempt to get closer to the non-reachable ideal of justice in law through competitive presentations before impartial judges, juries, and arbitrators. Many of the complaints come, as was described previously, from legal theorists, others from empirical researchers. Some of the complaints are simple statements of opinion: "This isn't the way things used to be done in the far better past." The majority of the complaints, however, rely on a counterallegation that has almost become a slogan: "The haves come out ahead."[36] And here, it must be admitted, the complainers do appear to have a valid point.

Richard Zitrin and Carol Langford provide a far more blunt and much less genteel description of how far out in front these "haves" have now come in their 1999 book *The Moral Compass of the American Lawyer*. Those two authors start their Chapter 3 with the account of a woman employee who had sued a large business firm for sexual harassment by one of the senior executives of that firm. Zitrin and Langford during their investigation of this incident met with the attorney representing that executive. They then openly expressed their view at that meeting that this attorney must have suspected that his client was indeed guilty because that attorney had defended this same executive twice before on exactly similar charges, and then recorded his statement about the way in which he would go about his third defense. Equality in the procedures had no part in his plans:

> "Our job is to protect our clients, not to dole out resources to light-weights who can't stick it out. Litigation is a war of attrition. Our firm has the resources, and our client can back us up. If we fight every case to the nth degree, give no quarter and offer nothing, our opponents will fold nine times out of ten. The tenth time they may roll the dice and go to court, but even then their chances are not much better than even, and there's always an appeal."[37]

Conclusion of the Chapter

What is the conclusion of chapter 4? Legal conformity—always obey the law—in our view provides a very decent second step in evaluating the decisions and actions of persons in managerial positions that benefit some individuals, groups, and organizations but harm others, or that recognize the rights of some of those same individuals, groups, and organizations but ignore the rights of others. It provides this very decent second step because: (a) the outcome of legal conformity can be claimed to be a common good—an orderly and productive society—and (b) the adjudication of the content of the law through judges and juries elected or appointed by society provides an impartial mechanism for the interpretation of the law leading toward that common good.

But, due to the difficulty in adjusting in meaningful ways to the underlying assumptions that (a) all contending parties in courtroom proceedings before impartial judges and juries have equal financial resources to employ competent law firms; and (b) that all competent law firms have equal knowledge, experience, skill, reach, and the funding needed to demonstrate that competence within an open courtroom before an impartial judge and jury, something more is needed.

Our candidate for this "something more" is personal integrity. Simply expressed personal integrity is the wholeness or completeness of an individual human being, and a large part of that wholeness or completeness is the active consideration of the well-being and rights of others. The positives and the problems of this very basic approach will be addressed in chapter 5.

CHAPTER 5

Applying the Evaluative Construct of Personal Integrity

R C2 Corporation of Oak Brook, Illinois, is one of a relatively new type of commercial organizations. They are a marketing specialist in the children's toy industry. As such, they neither invent nor manufacture the toys that they sell. Instead, they contract with large media companies and publishing houses for the rights to use popular characters conceived by others such as Big Bird, Winnie the Pooh, Bob the Builder, and Thomas the Tank Engine. RC2 then designs wooden or stuffed toys based upon those characters, contracts with low-cost manufacturers, primarily in China, to make them, ships the finished toys in low-cost container vessels to the United States and Europe, and distributes them through low-cost retail chains such Wal-Mart, K-Mart, and Toys R Us for the final sale to parents. It is a low-cost and high-volume business model that has been financially very successful:

> In the toy business, RC2 was the little company that could. Though much smaller and less prominent than Mattel and Hasbro, RC2 has grown steadily…thanks largely to a strategy of sewing up licensing deals with big name brands. Its revenues have risen from $213 million in 2002 to $519 million least year [2006].[1]

The approving words above, however, were from the lead paragraph in an article announcing that the US Consumer Product Safety Commission (CPSC) had ordered RC2 Corporation to recall 1.5 million Thomas and Friends wooden railway train sets that consisted of model engines, cars, and track sections because their paint coatings contained lead. The CPSC did not disclose the actual lead content in the recalled toys. But a commission spokesperson said that RC2's Chinese manufacturer appeared to have substituted highly leaded pigments for some portion of the lead-free paint the corporation had specified.

Parents, of course, were surprised and shocked. Lead is known to be highly toxic. When ingested by young children, it can cause learning disabilities, behavioral problems, and growth concerns. In older children and adults, lead poisoning can lead to high blood pressure, kidney failure, and stomach distress. The highly adverse effects of lead upon health had become generally known during the 1960s, and laws were passed in the early 1970s throughout the United States and Western Europe to restrict lead amounts in all consumer products, and over time these laws had been extended on a nearly global basis. By 2007, for example, it was illegal in China to use lead-based paint on export goods. Despite the parental concerns and the relevant laws, however, lead paint continued to be found on many children's toys. Part of the problem was the lack of resources within the CPSC to conduct inspections either at foreign plants or domestic sites.

> The Consumer Products Safety Commission has safety standards, but it has only 100 field investigators and compliance personnel nationwide to conduct inspections at ports, warehouses and stores of $22 billion worth of toys and tens of billions of dollars' worth of other consumer product sold in the country each year.[2]

What went wrong? It was easy to blame the Chinese toy-manufacturing companies, and many people did. They explained that lead paint creates brighter, shinier colors that appeal both to the children who play with the toys and the parents who purchase them. Also, lead paint flows more evenly, so that it is easier and less expensive to apply. And finally, lead paint is much cheaper; it is said to sell in China for a third of the cost of paint that would meet global standards of protection. The general conclusion of those on this side of "it's their fault" argument was that the Chinese manufacturers had deliberately disregarded both the standards in their purchase contracts and the laws in their country in search of higher profits.

Others, however, disagreed with that view. Members of this group believed that the responsibility extended far beyond the Chinese manufacturers to companies within both the United States and Western

Europe. These critics pointed to a recent change in the competitive structure of the children's toy industry in both of those regions. Traditionally, this industry had three participants: small manufacturing companies who designed and made the toys, regional wholesale firms who distributed the toys, and local retail stores who sold the toys. These toys were almost always generic; that is, they were of the "If you've seen one stuffed bear, cast truck, or wooden locomotive you've seen them all" variety.

Similar to many other industries, however, the children's toy industry began to consolidate in search of the dual economies of scale and of scope during the 1980s. This was at the same time that children's television programs such as Sesame Street began to dominate the networks with content that was both intriguing to preschool children and acceptable to their parents. The right to market toys based upon the characters popularized on those programs quickly was recognized as a huge competitive advantage by the media companies who held the rights to those characters, the manufacturers who wanted those rights for their toys, and the retail chains who wanted the high volume sales that would result.

The small manufacturers, who over this period had only grown by slow accretions, were caught between large and well-financed media companies who wanted high royalties for the rights to make toys based upon their popular characters, and the equally large and well-financed retail chains who wanted low costs to boost their profits when selling these toys at consumer-attractive prices.

Numerous accounts have been published relating the experiences of manufacturers who had submitted a proposal to supply a given consumer product to one of those massive retail chains. The usual response by most chains was to invite sales representatives of the manufacturer to meet with purchasing agents of the chain at their headquarters office. The headquarters office of the largest and best-known retail chain was located in a rural section of a southwestern state. Once there, the sales representatives of the manufacturer most frequently were told by the purchasing agents of the chain that their analytical staff had examined the costs of producing the items listed on that company's proposal in the volumes that would be needed to satisfy demand, and concluded not by negotiating the price but by stating: "This is the price (a specific dollar figure) that we're willing to pay and that you're going to have to accept."

There are far fewer anecdotal accounts of manufacturers going similarly hat in hand to the headquarter offices of the large media companies (generally in metropolitan New York or Los Angeles, not in rural Arkansas) for the right to make a product—either items of clothing or toys—that had become popular through widespread exposure on television. It can be assumed, however, that once there they encountered a similar, though perhaps not quite so brusque, "This is the royalty you're going to have to pay" rigidity. There was very limited bargaining at either end of the value chain in the consolidated children's toy industry because both the media companies and the retail chains, equally large and well-financed participants, held nearly complete pricing power.

The small manufacturers, given those imposed demands on the royalties they had to pay and the prices they had to accept, quickly arranged for far less expensive production overseas and turned themselves into marketing specialists. This substantial change in the competitive structure of the preschool children's toy industry, from the traditional to the consolidated, took place over a limited number of years, and is shown in figure 5.1.

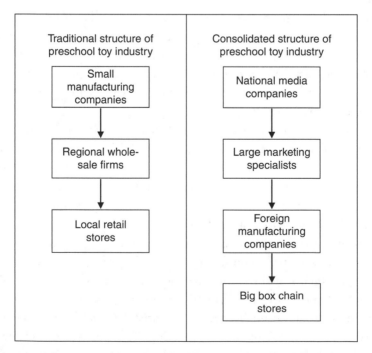

Figure 5.1 Traditional versus consolidated structures of the preschool children's toy industry.

In the *traditional* structure of the preschool children's toy industry, lead paint was never found to have been used on children's toys once the harmful impacts of lead became well known and the laws prohibiting its use were passed. In the *consolidated* structure of this industry, however, the use of lead paint apparently became very common very fast, despite that knowledge and those laws. What changed? Why did this happen?

It was easy to place the blame on the Chinese manufacturers. They were the added members of the value chain, the "new kids" on this particular block. They were also the first non-Western members of the chain, with unfamiliar goals, norms, beliefs, and values. And, most importantly, they were the most closely involved member who actually purchased the lead paint from their suppliers, directed their employees to apply this coating to the wooden toys destined for the United States and Western Europe, and ignored the explicit contract terms from the marketing specialist firms forbidding its use. Does any blame at all attach to the other three members of this value chain under those conditions? In our view, it certainly does. Managers at those other three members did not anticipate what could go so drastically wrong so very quickly as a result of their own stringent pricing demands.

Anticipating Problems before They Occur

Up to this point in the discussion, we have focused upon the responsibility of managers within for-profit, non-profit, or governmental organizations to: (a) continually evaluate the balance of benefits and harms, and the comparison of rights recognized and rights ignored, that come from their own decisions and actions or from those of other managers within their own organization; and (b) to be continually prepared (but not required) to fully explain the legitimacy (the supportive principles and/or accepted rules or standards) of the remedial decisions or actions they felt were needed. But many times now managers in one of the participants within a horizontal joint venture or vertical value chain have found that the harms to their own careers, their own organizations, and their own societies have come not from within their own organization but from the unanticipated decisions and actions of managers in other participating firms within that joint venture or value chain that were allegedly cooperating to produce a joint product and achieve a common goal. This is exactly what happened at the blowout, explosion, and fire of the Deepwater Horizon recounted in chapter 1, in the financial collapse of the residential housing and mortgage securitization industries recounted in chapter 3, and here in the mass production of children's toys based upon popular cartoon characters for sale to large chain retailers that has been explained previously in this chapter.

The problem is how can managers in one organization become aware of the potentially harmful—even potentially disastrous—decisions being made and actions taking place by managers at other allegedly interdependent firms within the same cooperative structure? Our argument is that they can be guided in their search by looking at the assumptions, omissions, and weak spots in the evaluative constructs that have already been discussed of economic efficiency and legal conformity, and in those that soon will be discussed of personal integrity. Here are some questions that probably should be asked:

1. *Competitive markets:* Are all of the intercompany exchange markets within the full horizontal joint venture or complete vertical value chain adequately competitive? When one or more companies hold dominant power in promotion, distribution, or pricing there can be either exploitive actions by the companies that hold that power and/or adaptive reactions by those who don't. It seems such an obvious recommendation, but perhaps managers in all firms should understand the degree of competition in all of the markets in which they are engaged, and look for exploitive actions or adaptive reactions that may harm the well-being and rights of others when the stabilizing consequences of full competition are absent.

2. *Informed participants:* Are all of the participants in the intercompany exchange markets within the full horizontal joint venture or complete vertical value chain adequately informed? When either sellers or buyers lack adequate information, there are advantages that can be exploited or mistakes that can be made, as both certainly were in the residential mortgage industry. Again it would seem to be an obvious recommendation, but perhaps here also managers should understand the extent of information held by the participants in all of the markets in which they are engaged, and look for exploitive actions on one side and unfortunate reactions on the other when the stabilizing consequences of full information are absent.

3. *External costs:* Have the potential external costs of the full horizontal joint venture or vertical value chain been identified, estimated, and included in the pricing? This is the most difficult question. It is also

the most common problem. We hope that readers have noticed that in all of the disasters that we have described—and let us once again explain that we do not think that "disaster" is too strong a word for these events, including the impact of ingested lead upon the mental and physical development of an unknown number of preschool children—the individuals, groups, and organizations who had nothing to do with the decisions and actions of the managers who brought about those events were among the most harmed by the outcomes. *Let us quickly add—and also let us strongly emphasize—that in our view almost all of those managerial decisions and actions that led to these disasters were not deliberate actions intended to harm others. Instead they were mistaken choices made to benefit themselves.*

They were mistaken choices because the previously described forces of: (a) the expanding intensity of competition; (b) the advancing complexity of technology; and (c) the dominating advantage of innovation had brought new products, processes, markets, methods, and materials. As a result, there were no historical data sets upon which to base reliable estimates of the statistical probability of occurrence and the financial value of impact for each of a range of potential outcomes of a given decision or action, and therefore the commonly relied upon risk/return ratios could not be computed. Under these conditions, which have become so much more common today, there is no obvious recommendation for us to make in forecasting external costs beyond the proposal that managers in for-profit, non-profit, and governmental organization rely much more heavily upon individual imagination (what can happen) and personal integrity (what should be done).

Definition of Personal Integrity

"Personal integrity" refers to the completeness or wholeness of a human being. The root words, of course, are "integer," which refers to a whole number, and "integral," which means a single unit of related parts. When we say that a given individual "has integrity," we mean that such a person comes complete with a interrelated set of goals, norms, beliefs, and values that together make up the character of that person, and that character does not vary over time, with conditions or under temptations. In short, integrity in a person means that what you see in his or her character is what you're going to get in his or her decisions and actions.

Personal integrity, as such, goes far beyond the behavioral standards of being honest, telling the truth, and keeping one's word. Here we would like to repeat the analogy that we gave earlier in chapter 2. We apologize for the repetition but we believe that it provides the best understanding we can convey of the "wider than normally accepted" range of the very basic evaluative construct of personal integrity.

If the authors of this book, in the analogy we earlier provided and are slightly embarrassed now to repeat, openly said that we were going to hire young children to handle toxic chemicals at low wages under appalling conditions in a foreign country where the output markets were rapidly growing but the relevant laws were painfully weak, and then we went ahead and did exactly that, we might claim that we had acted honestly, spoken truthfully, and kept our respective words, but we doubt that many people would consider us to be persons of high integrity. Personal integrity at the absolute base in a managerial context depends upon *a manager's active and respectful consideration of the well-being and rights for other people associated in some way—as owners, employees, customers, distributors, suppliers, owners, neighbors, or members of society—with the organization at which that manager is employed.*

Theory-Based Construct for Personal Integrity

The question is, then, what principles should be cited, what standards should be observed, or what rules should be followed to evaluate this active and respectful consideration of the distribution of benefits, the allocation of harms, and the recognition of rights for the people associated in some way with the firm that many if not most of those people would agree to be right and just and fair or—our preferred term again—legitimate. We need a theory-based methodology that can be said to be universal (applicable to everyone), absolute (with exceptions for no one), impartial (without favoritism for any one), and basic (understandable by all).

We have a candidate for such a theory-based methodology that will perform that evaluative function and meet those needed criteria. That candidate is moral rationality. Moral philosophers have—over millennia, not just centuries—developed a series of normative rules for conduct that they believed to be universal, absolute, impartial, and basic, and thus could be used to construct compelling arguments in support of what has generally been termed the "common good." These rules, when shorn of their frequently lengthy theoretical justifications, have often been condensed into what many now term ethical principles of analysis that are alleged to logically separate right from wrong in the actions of individuals, groups, and organizations. That is, they are often said to define the characteristics of a decision that makes the resulting action and its consequential outcome truly right or truly wrong.

Let us quickly add that we disagree with this proposed "truly right or truly wrong" capability of the evaluative process of moral rationality because—as we have stated so many time before in this discourse—we believe that it is impossible to adequately define the very basic contrasts of right versus wrong, or of their commonly associated synonyms of just versus unjust or fair versus unfair. There are simply far too many different types and degrees of benefits and harms, far too many different forms and priorities of rights and wrongs, and far too many different variations in the self-interest, organizational-interest, and social-interest priority rankings of people to reach any ethical principle capable of making universal, absolute, impartial, and understandable right versus wrong judgments about managerial decisions or actions and their consequential outcomes.

Here, of all things, we find ourselves in full agreement with a number of current moral philosophers of considerable stature who also object to the use of ethical principles of analysis to separate the right actions of individuals, groups, or organizations that add to the alleged common good from the wrong actions by those same actors that subtract from that frequently used but imprecisely defined goal joining societal well-being and orderly existence. These objections of active scholars come from their conviction that ethical principles may be universal and absolute in the sense of being logically applicable to everyone and with exemptions for no one at a certain time in history, but not in the sense of extending over the evolving periods of history. That is, advocates of this point of view—and they are by no means a small minority among active moral philosophers—maintain that *absolute ethical principles and objective moral truths simply don't exist in a world that is undergoing rapid economic, social, and technological change.*

Members of this "the actualities of right versus wrong change over time" group of scholars believe that ethical principles are more behavioral norms that might have seemed relevant at one point and place in global history, but that appear to have become irrelevant when that point and that place have passed. This viewpoint has perhaps best been expressed by Richard Rorty, at the time president of the American Philosophical Association, who at a meeting of applied ethicists made the following argument, which was then published for wider distribution in an applied ethics journal:

We think that adding "absolute" to "wrong" or "objective" to "truth" is an empty rhetorical gesture. It is just a way of pounding on the podium... When decisions get tough, invoking notions like "absolute-ness" or "objectivity" does nothing to make them easier.[3]

We agree with Prof. Rorty that the really tough decisions don't yield to normative notions of universality or absoluteness, but, suppose we look at these ethical principles of analysis not as time-dependent means of establishing rigid distinctions between right and wrong, but as amazingly deep insights into the complex nature of partially self-centered, partially organization-centered (family, clan, or tribe in days past, generally the employer in days present), and partially society-centered (town, province, or kingdom in the past; city, state, or nation in the present) nature of actual human beings, and ask what principle, rule, or standard can serve to begin to meld those competing allegiances.

Supporters of both the "optimal profit between impartial mar-kets" theory of economics and the "zealous advocacy before impar-tial deciders" theory of law do not believe that this melding is needed. They assume that, while a limited number of people may well be more outward-focused than inward-oriented, the large majority is definitely on the inward-oriented—or, more bluntly stated, purely self-seeking—side. That large majority is dominant, supporters of both of these theory-based evaluative processes claim, and thus fully validates their theoretical claims that the self-interested choices of individual consumers, suppliers, and citizens actually do, given the impartial choices of self-centered purchas-ers in competitive input and output markets and the impartial decisions of duty-bound judges, juries, and arbitrators in open court and hearing rooms, constrain the decisions and actions of managers, and thus improve the well-being and expand the rights of all individuals, groups, and orga-nizations within a given society.

But suppose we make the reverse assumption, and start from the pro-posal that, while some people are totally self-centered, a large majority is not, and that what we need is a means to bring the interests of those latter individuals much more fully into the evaluations of the managerial decisions and actions that benefit some while harming others, or that rec-ognize the rights of some while ignoring the rights of others. As you read more about the ethical principles that have been proposed over the mil-lennia, allegedly to define the differences between right and wrong acts or between just and unjust outcomes, you will find that the principles can be interpreted as *proposing the alleged characteristics of managerial decisions and actions that should bring about lesser conflict and greater cooperation among the individuals, groups, and organizations that make up our full society.* This latter, we believe, almost everyone will agree to be a decent and desirable goal.

The Nature of Moral Philosophy

If you are willing to accept for now our interpretation that the true nature of the ethical principles that have been proposed by moral philosophers from the fifth century BC to the twenty-first century AD was much more to lessen the destructive conflicts and to forward the cooperative efforts within society because those behaviors would lead indirectly but definitely toward that unreachable but approachable goal of the Common Good, then we believe that the very real contributions of those noted scholars will be much clearer to you.

Our belief is that the ethical principles that these scholars have developed over the millennia *focus on providing the underlying rationale for the interest in and the concern over the well-being and rights of other people that does exist—to sharply varying degrees—in the character of almost all rational human beings.* None of those scholars in our view were stating: "This is what everyone *must do* to improve the well-being and recognize the rights of others within society." Instead, each of them, again in our view, was suggesting: "This is what everyone *can do* to reduce the conflict and improve the cooperation within our society, which will result in improving the well-being and expanding the rights for all."

Let us summarize our basic argument here before moving from this chapter segment on the nature of moral philosophy to the next chapter segment on the relevant principles of moral philosophers:

1. *Emotional appeals*: Our first point is that the conceptual ideals of rightness, justice, and fairness have powerful emotional appeals. These ideals may not be definable, but they constitute an important part of almost everyone's vocabulary, and a basis for almost everyone's thinking. The declarative "That's not fair!" is not limited just to four-year olds in discussing the relative size of ice-cream servings.

2. *Legitimacy needs*: Our second point is that these indefinable but relevant ideals, in order to be effective in changing decisions, actions, attitudes, and behaviors, need legitimacy: a set of clearly stated, easily understood, and generally recognized principles and their derived rules and standards to provide a basis for declarative judgments. Four-year

olds lack those principles, and are just at the edge of beginning to learn the rules and the standards.

3. *Legitimacy outcomes*: Our third point is that these easily understood and generally recognized principles, and their derived rules and standards, *when clearly stated* bring about the perception of rightness, justice, and fairness. We can't, given the varying degrees of personal-interest, organizational-interest, and societal-interest that exist among individuals, achieve generally accepted definitions of those terms, but logically supported perceptions among large numbers of people come awfully close.

4. *Perception results*: Our last point, and this is the one we most wish to convey, is that these *perceptions* of just treatment among individuals from different economic and social situations and from different cultural and religious traditions, *logically* should result in the decreased conflict and increased cooperation that is so needed in our competitively intense, technologically complex, and socially contentious world. *Empirically* is a different matter. That will be discussed in chapter 6.

Relevant Principles of Moral Philosophers

We have earlier defined personal integrity as the "active and respectful consideration of the well-being and rights of other people." We have proposed to evaluate the extent or degree of personal integrity evidenced by individuals in managerial positions by applying the ethical principles of moral philosophers. But, we are not going to make use of all of the ethical principles that have been proposed by moral philosophers over the centuries. Some—Bentham,[4] Mill,[5] and Smith[6]—focus on the most basic needs for sustenance and the role of individual choice in meeting those needs; their ideas have evolved into the evaluative construct of economic efficiency, which has already been addressed in chapter 3. Others—Hobbes[7] and Locke[8]—focus on the most basic rights of life, liberty, and property and the place of governments in protecting those rights. Their ideas are now contained in the evaluative construct of legal conformity, which was covered in chapter 4. We wish to focus on the most basic duties owned to others; these are the character traits that we term personal integrity, and are the subject of this segment of the chapter.

There are seven ethical principles that we believe are relevant to the *duties* of individuals in managerial positions whose decisions and actions can impact, in both positive and negative ways, the well-being and rights of others. We expect to describe, briefly, the historical conditions at the time that the principle was first proposed; the supportive rationale for that principle; and finally a brief statement of our interpretation of that principle in question format. Following that interpretation we should like to ask our readers, after they finish reading each of the entries that we bellieve to be relevant to personal integrity to consider three very basic questions:

1. Would the particular ethical principle whose description you have just finished reading help *you* in logically defining the characteristics that bring about *your* perception of rightness, justice, and fairness in managerial decisions and actions?

2. Would this same ethical principle whose description you have just finished reading help *you* in logically convincing *others* that the managerial decision or action that you recommend could legitimately be viewed as being right and just and fair?

3. Would this same ethical principle whose description you have just finished reading, if used widely throughout *your* society, help to increase the cooperative efforts and reduce the continuing conflicts within your society?

In short, our belief is that if you find these ethical principles helpful in logically deciding what you perceive to be right and just and fair, and a contributor to the common good as you understand that elusive but essential goal, then maybe others will also. If others do also, then perhaps you can justify your managerial decisions and actions in ways that reduce conflict, increase cooperation, and thus benefit you, your organization, and your society.

There are, in our view, seven ethical principles that have been proposed over the past 2,500 years that we believe to be directly relevant to the evaluative construct of personal integrity. In order to emphasize the lack of a normative "everyone must act this way" insistence and instead stress the presence of a descriptive "what do you think" orientation of each of these principles, we are going to summarize the historical conditions and the supportive logic for each, and then express our conclusion on these gradually evolving principles, rules, or standards in question, not statement, format. Now, after this lengthy discussion of the interpretation of the ethical principles relevant to the evaluative construct of personal integrity, let us move on to the actuality of those principles.

The Principle of Self-Interests (Protagoras, 490–420 BC and Democritus, 460–370 BC)

The issue addressed by these early Greek philosophers was the question: "What constitutes a good life? That is, what should a man (women were not considered important enough in Athenian society to be included in the political discussions that took place in the public "male only" forums, and thus were also excluded from philosophical attention) strive for?" Only fragments of their original writings remain, but these twin questions on the nature of a good life and the goal of a good citizen were clearly predominant. The most famous surviving quotation of Protagoras is "Man is the measure of all things."[9] This referred to man, not men, and the usual interpretation is that the only measure that matters is the life of the individual, and the means by which that life can be made to be satisfying. For years, the most famous surviving quotation of Democritus was thought to be "Better a good life than a pleasant dinner," and the common interpretation here was that it was only the long-term goal of a good life, to be evaluated just prior to death, that really mattered, but now the authenticity of that short but memorable phrase has been not just strongly questioned but solidly refuted. The general theme that money and authority do not count in the evaluation of a good life, however, remained fully embedded at the center of this pre-Socratic approach to living, with the notion that satisfaction in one's life just prior to death was the critical issue. A less memorably stated but more fully accepted Democritus quotation demonstrating this point is: "It is not great sums of money or a mass of possessions, nor even certain political offices and powers, which produce happiness and blessedness, but rather freedom and gentleness in our feelings and a disposition of soul which measures out what is natural."[10]

Both of these ancient writers agreed that the evaluative goals for that good life had to be a combination of comfortable conditions and cheerful companions, and that such untroubled happiness could be achieved only by a moderation in personal lifestyles and an acceptance of public standards. Both those conditions were thought to be necessary in order to avoid irritating or provoking others. Justice was thus seen as a contract in which each citizen agreed not to harm other citizens, either by acting adversely to them or by creating envy among them, and it was proposed that all parties would accept this contract because it was in everyone's *long-term self-interests* to live in a peaceful, orderly society with little probability of retribution and vengeful harm.

Here we find that 2,500 years ago, two very early philosophers were discussing a universal principle that would tie good personal conduct to the goal of a stable, cooperative society, and they were using the *long-term* consequences of that conduct as the basis for this principle. Hopefully it is now clearer what was meant by earlier statements in this text that ethical principles have to be applicable to everyone, with exceptions for no one, without favoritism for any one, and logically understandable by all. In our view, this ancient principle clearly would have been seen as applicable to every Athenian citizen qualified to attend one of the public forums within that city, without exception from and impartial among all those qualified to be there, and understandable by everybody in attendance. The central question to ask yourself as you apply this "leading toward less conflict and more cooperation" principle, rule, or standard to a decision or action you face is "Does the decision or action that I and the members of my group or organization are currently considering advance our long-term, *enlightened* self-interests, or does it damage those interests by ignoring the rights or harming the well-being of other individuals, groups, or organizations who may consequently ignore our rights or harm our well-being when they first find the opportunity?"

Principle of Personal Virtues (Socrates, 470–399 BC; Plato, 427–347 BC; and Aristotle, 384–322 BC)

The concept of moderated or enlightened self-interest was not acceptable to this remarkable trio of Greek philosophers. The problem, Socrates noted early in his series of public discussions or forum teachings, was that a person could ignore the rights and harm the well-being of others and then quickly reach a position of such wealth and power that he would have no fear of future retribution from the people he had harmed upon the way. His "Ring of Gyges" fable provided an illustrative example of a poor shepherd who found a ring that made him invisible whenever he wished, and he was able to use that capability to kill the king, marry the queen, and totally ignore the opposition of his countrymen.[11]

Socrates built upon this example by starting a different method of analysis to which all three moral philosophers contributed, and that ended with Aristotle's principle that everyone should act in ways that conveyed a sense of honor, pride, and self-worth. We don't necessarily have to be kind and considerate to others, they as a group concluded. We don't even have to be concerned about the reactions of others. We do, however, have to be honest, truthful, courageous, and just in our interactions with others for our own benefit. Why? Because the goal of human existence is the *active, rational pursuit of excellence*, and excellence requires an extended version of that combination of personal virtues.[12]

Let us explain, at this early stage of the discussion of Classical Greek philosophy, that we believe that it helps greatly in understanding the sequential writings of these three overlapping scholars if one knows at the start where Aristotle would wind up at the end. Aristotle did not emphasize the term "excellence" in his writings. Instead he referred to "the pursuit of happiness," but then quickly admitted that there was much disagreement about the meaning of that term. For many, he explained, happiness meant living well and acting well.[13] Cruder people, he continued, claimed that happiness was pursuing pleasure.[14] The more refined, he explained, said that happiness was public honor[15] and/or personal nobility.[16] He himself appeared to conclude early in the *Nicomachean Ethics* text that happiness was "a certain activity of soul [the character of the individual] in accord with perfect virtue,"[17] but then waited until close to the end before expanding strongly on his concept of "perfect virtue":

> If happiness is an activity in accord with virtue, it is reasonable that it would accord with the most excellent virtue, and this would be the virtue belonging to what is best…and that this activity is contemplative, it has been said.[18]

> For this activity [contemplation] is the most excellent one; the intellect is the most excellent of the things in us, and the things with which the intellect is concerned are the most excellent of the things that can be known.[19]

Thus, we do not believe that it constitutes a misrepresentation to change Aristotle's goal of a proper life from "accordance with perfect virtue" to the "rational pursuit of excellence." We have made this change because we believe that this "rational pursuit of excellence"—a goal also often termed "knowledge of the good"[20]—is the basis of Classic Greek philosophy. If you commit firmly those two phrases to your memory, then much of the rest of the teachings of Socrates, Plato, and Aristotle will be far clearer to you. This is particularly true for Plato, the second in this sequence, whose writings tend to be far more metaphorical and further reaching than the other two. And, if you think seriously about the meaning that those three men together placed upon what they believed to be the interrelated spheres of politics as rules for the conduct of society and of ethics as goals for the conduct of its members,[21] then you might well find a new respect for the constructs of both politics and ethics, a respect that, we fear, has greatly deteriorated over the past few years. But now, back to the conceptual progression from Socrates to Plato to Aristotle, and—particularly—to the causal conditions that existed in Athens at that time.

In Athens, 2,400 years ago, these three perspicacious men began to address questions of ethical duties and moral justice, and laid the foundation for the Western approach to both politics (again, for well-deserved emphasis, *rules for the conduct of society*) and ethics (also again, for equally well-deserved emphasis, *goals for the conduct of its members*). This sort of thinking about duties and justice, about politics and ethics, had never before existed in the ancient world. Why in Athens, and why at this time?

The reason was an unusual combination of prosperity and peace. Greece is a mountainous peninsula, with limited agricultural land that was suitable for growing substantial amounts of grain, but the climate was warm and mild, ideal for olives, grapes, and livestock. There were easy "along the coast" sea routes to Egypt, then the granary of the Eastern Mediterranean. Egypt had surplus wheat and barley for export, but needed olive oil and wine for home consumption. A very prosperous trade developed between the two regions. The defeat of the invading Persian army at Marathon in 490 BC brought a period of peace in Greece that lasted for 140 years, a time that came to be known as the "Golden Age" of Athens.

Conflicts between the nobles (the ex-warriors), the merchants (the ex-sailors), and the citizens (the residents who were qualified by wealth, by birth, or by reputation to participate in the public forums) brought about an interest in government within Athens. An interest in government brought about what were termed schools but were more properly adult education classes, first to teach rhetoric (how to talk to assembled groups of citizens), and then logic (how to convince members of those assembled groups). An interest in logic led back to the question, "What is the good life?"

Socrates addressed this question, "What is the good life," for both individuals and societies, which, at the time, meant economically advanced city-states such as Athens. Socrates wrote nothing, yet Plato is generally credited with recording Socrates' discussions with other Athenians in the form of a set of dialogues soon after the death of the older man, and these can thus be assumed to be Socrates' thoughts if not his words. Some recent scholars disagree, however. They claim that Plato used the dialogues as a means of expressing his own beliefs. This all happened 2,400 years ago. It is impossible to be certain today, especially given that the two men were exceedingly similar in their goals if not in their beliefs.

The goal of Socrates, assuming that the dialogues were indeed his thoughts, was to develop the "first rule for a successful life." Successful at this time meant happy; a term that probably then would have been translated as contented and prosperous. Socrates argued, however, that there could be no happiness in the pursuit of pleasure, or in the ownership of property, unless you knew how to use each one of those well. Knowledge of the "good"—meaning knowledge of what indeed is good in pleasure and property—was thus the goal of life. It was necessary, Socrates concluded, to develop both so that everyone—nobles, merchants, and citizens alike, but not it has to be admitted the indentured servants and enslaved laborers who made up 5/6ths of the population—could participate. Athens at this time was a democracy of the privileged, and it was felt that these were the people who needed to recognize proposals that were good both for their character (ethics) and for their society (politics). Ethics and politics, once again, were believed to be synonymous in Classic Greek thinking; you essentially could not have one without the other. We hope that readers will excuse us for adding, "Would that this were still so."

Plato succeeded Socrates as the major public thinker following the death of the older man in 399 BC. Plato focused on politics, on the need to have a good society in order for citizens to have good lives. He wrote *The Republic,* in which he began discussing the concept of justice, what it was and how it could be achieved. To ensure clarity it is going to be necessary to repeat here what was explained earlier that Athens, unlike the other city-states on the Greek peninsula, was divided into statesmen (the most prominent of the citizens; they were the men of thought who were to direct the state), soldiers (the ex-warriors, they were the men of courage who were to protect the state), and merchants (the ex-sailors, they were the men of property who were to supply the state). You needed all three for a good (again, contented and prosperous) society. "Justice" was defined as the harmonious union of all three groups, with each group excelling at what they did best, and with no one group interfering with the activities of either of the other groups.[22]

Aristotle, the third in this remarkable sequence, focused on ethics, on the need to have good citizens in order to form a good society. The goal of a society, he wrote, had to be happiness for all of the citizens. But what is happiness if not pleasure, wealth, or fame? Our interpretation, as we explained previously, is that Aristotle concluded that happiness comes from excellence in the character of those citizens. Such excellence, he continued, could be found along a number of different dimensions of personal character, termed virtues, with the choice of the position selected for each dimension combining reason and thought. This combination of reason and thought Aristotle latter termed deliberation.[23]

What were these character dimensions, these personal virtues, with the proper position selected through deliberation? *Courage* in conflict was one, with the deliberative choice coming midway between recklessness and cowardice. *Moderation* in pleasures was another, with the choice here midway between licentiousness and insensibility. *Liberality* with money was the third, with the choice midway between prodigality and stinginess. The conclusion in this last instance was that the money could be used badly at either extreme, but well toward the center.[24]

Magnificence was worthy expenditures on great things, a deliberative choice between ostentation and parsimony. It primarily was spending not on one's self but on common needs. *Greatness of soul* was self-esteem, with the choice between being vain and being timid. A reasoned and thoughtful rule here was that a virtuous man should care more for the truth than for public opinion. *Ambition* was focused on the desire for honor, and the reasoned and thoughtful rule here was that a virtuous man should never strive for more honor than was deserved.[25]

This is somewhat of an aside, but our view is that all three of that last group of virtues—magnificence, greatness of soul, and ambition—could be far more understandably encompassed under the single personal characteristic of *pride*: pride in what one had accomplished, pride in how one had acted, and pride in the limits that one had set on the rewards one received. Now, back to Aristotle's own listing of personal virtues.

Gentleness, he suggested, was a controlled response to perceived harms; it was marked by a desire to be calm, and resolve issues by reason, not by passion. Friendliness was a controlled association with other citizens, midway between being obsequious (praising everyone and opposing nothing) and being quarrelsome (opposing everything and praising no one). Truthfulness was the only virtue in Aristotle's listing that had no preferred middle ground. The rule here was simple and direct: "A man should guard against what is false on the grounds that it is shameful."[26]

The next to the last of the virtues Aristotle listed was *wittiness*. This might seem to be irrelevant to virtue because of the usual connection of that term with mildly amusing speech, but Aristotle explained that what he had in mind was not buffoonery or boorish behavior, but tact. And tact, speaking in a form thought not to annoy, he concluded was essential for the decent person.[27]

The last of the virtues Aristotle listed was *justice*. He had the same difficulty defining this term as have all the rest of us, from his day to our own. Aristotle's first attempt was to equate just behavior with lawful behavior, but soon saw the major defect there "in the case of the law laid down haphazardly."[28] His conclusion was: (a) that justice was a combination of all the virtues, saying justice "is complete because he who possesses it is able to use virtue in relation to another, and not only as regards himself[29]; and (b) that justice in personal behavior was related to politics because "We say that those things apt to produce and preserve happiness for the political community are in a manner just."[30]

In summary, we can say that in Aristotle's view a member of the political class, one who was deemed worthy of attending the public forums held for public deliberations and decisions as either a statesman, a soldier, or a merchant, should be courageous, moderate, and tactful in his relationships with other people, careful with the use of his money for personal wants and public expenditures, proud of what he had done, proud of how he had acted, and proud of the limits he had set upon his rewards.

This is not a bad principle, or set of standards and rules, for personal conduct, even for those of us that are not now statesmen, soldiers, or merchants, particularly as that principle, standard, or rule is justified by its alleged contribution toward general happiness and the common good. That is, if everyone would strive for true excellence, not just casual betterment, along the 11 dimensions of perfect behavior that Aristotle had established, then there would be less conflict and more cooperation between the political groups, each with different goals, norms, beliefs, and values that Plato had noted in his perfect republic. And, this is clearly a principle, standard, or rule that today can be said to be applicable to everyone, with exception for no one, without favoritism for any one, and understandable by all, and is not thus limited just to the members of the governing class. Those were the only ones who mattered in the ancient Greek democracy.

Before moving on to our conclusion regarding this very early but very important contribution to an understanding of the nature of personal integrity—the unity or wholeness of the character of individual persons—we should briefly like to comment on Aristotle's apparent omission of honesty as one of his 11 virtues, of the 11 ways he believed citizens should act to achieve excellence. He did include it, but only as an afterthought. In his comments about justice he noted that "To be just in transactions [selling, buying, lending] it is necessary to be equal in relation to something and to certain persons, with the same equity for each.[31] He then again connected politics and ethics:

> In communities concerned with exchange, the just in this sense—reciprocity in accord with proportion and in accord with equity—hold them together, for the city stays together by proportional reciprocity.[32]

How do we convert Aristotle's proposal for excellence in personal characteristics as determined by deliberative choices along 12 virtue dimensions (the original 11 plus honesty), and as supported by Plato's proposal for justice in political decisions, into a simpler principle, standard, or rule for everyday use in the twenty-first century? We believe—and this is the pleasure of working with the sequence of Aristotle, Plato, and Aristotle for their eventual conclusions are far more definite than their frequent wanderings—that to be fairly simple: "We should all be open, honest, truthful, moderate, and proud of what we do so that we can all work together for the benefit of all." This has frequently been translated into simplified terms, and we will use those terms for the question we would suggest you ask yourself: "Does the decision or action that I and members of my group or organization are now considering damage the rights or harm the well-being of other individuals, groups, or organizations and, if so, have we been open, honest, and truthful about those potential impacts, and would we feel proud and honored were our causal actions and those harmful impacts become widely known?"

The Principle of Religious Injunctions
(Early Religious Writers of Numerous Faiths)

The problem with the "be open, honest, truthful, and proud" rule, which clearly can be applied to everyone, with exceptions for no one, without favoritism for any, and understandable by all is that these personal virtues are not enough. There are many people who can be open, honest, truthful, and even proud of decisions and actions that many of the rest of us would view as exploitive, mean, and excessively self-centered. Something more was felt to be needed, even at the time of Socrates, Plato, and Aristotle, and for many of the early religious writers that something more came from the inherent and established concepts of community (brotherhood and sisterhood) and service (kindness, compassion, and help) that underlie almost all faiths.

It is always awkward to write of religious faiths, and of their injunctions to act with kindness and compassion in service to others, in a more broadly focused book because, obviously, faiths do differ, and unfortunately in the past and continuing into the present those differences have been more emphasized than the similarities, and the results have been war, oppression, inhumanity, and death.

But, there are definite similarities between the faiths. Let us give a series of examples. Variations of the well-known "Do unto others as you would have others do unto you" Golden Rule of Christianity can be found in almost all of the other religions of the world,[33] and many of these predate by a considerable extent the beginning of the Christian era. These are described below in alphabetic order so as not to imply priority or precedence:

- Buddhism (religious creed and ethical system of central and eastern Asia, founded about 460 BC). "Hurt not others in ways that you yourself would find hurtful."[34]
- Christianity (religious creed founded in Judea before the year AD 1). The St. Matthew version is "In everything do to others as you would have others do to you; for this is the law and the prophets."[35] The St. Luke version: "Do to others as you would have them do to you."[36]
- Confucianism (ethical system added to the existing Chinese religious creed about 510 BC). "What you do not want done to yourself do not do to others."[37]
- Islam (religious creed of western and southeastern Asia, founded about AD 630). "No one is a true believer who does not prefer for his brother or his neighbor what he prefers for himself."[38]
- Judaism (religious creed founded by persons living on the eastern shore of the Mediterranean at a time estimated to be about 1,000 BC). "Do not do unto others what you would not have others do to you. This is the whole law, the rest merely commentaries upon it."[39]

- Paganism (a belief in multiple deities, each often with distinctive human characteristics, that began during the earliest existence of mankind and continued until relatively recent periods). A son of Zeus and Europa is said to have declared, "If he should suffer the things he did [to others], then justice would be straight."[40]
- Taoism (religious creed and philosophic system of northern China, founded about 550 BC). "Regard your neighbor's gain as your own gain, and regard your neighbor's loss as your own loss."[41]

The basic teachings of most religions, apparently derived from this primary rule that each person should treat others as he/she wished to be treated, also stress a sense of community among all holders of their given faith, a belief in a common goal for that community, and a duty of kindness, compassion, and help to all people, even to people outside that faith. Here we cannot cite quite so broad a set of sources as those shown above, but following from the examples of those sources we rather assume that the general content of the following statements, the first by St. Augustine (AD 354–430) and the second by St. Thomas Aquinas (1225–1274), is widely shared outside the Christian faith:

> Among those who are able to enjoy God with us, we love some whom we help, some by whom we are helped, some whose help we need and whose wants we supply, and some on whom we bestow no benefits and from whom we await none ourselves. Be that as it may, we should desire that all enjoy God with us and that all the assistance we give them or get from them should be directed to this end.[42]

> Again, the end of divine law is for man to cling to God. But one man may be aided to this end by another man, both in regard to knowledge and to love. For men are of mutual assistance to each other in the knowing of truth, and one may simulate another toward the good, and also restrain from evil.[43]

The modern version of this early ethical principle, once again applicable to all, with exception for no one, without favoritism for any one, and understandable by all, can be expressed in question form as: "Is the decision or action that I and others of my group or organization are now considering kind and compassionate toward others, and does it create a sense of community, a belief that all of us are working jointly toward a common goal of peace between and well-being for all?

The Principle of Universal Duties (Kant, 1724–1804)

One way of looking at the writings of Immanuel Kant is that he provides the rational support for the "do unto others" prescriptions that pervade so many religious faiths. This was not intentional. Kant was religious, but did not focus on religion in his writing.

Kant focused on the search for an absolute principle that would logically separate right from wrong in all human activities, but he wanted to base his reasoning on duties that are directly personal rather than outcomes that are indirectly consequential. Here we seem to be getting back to the non-definable constructs of right versus wrong, but read on a bit further. Kant started by proposing that nothing in this world could be considered to be an absolute good except for a goodwill.[44] This "goodwill" is usually translated as a person's beneficial desire or recognized duty to help others. Obviously a person's beneficial desire or recognized duty toward others cannot be directly observed because it is both internal and private.

How then can other people tell whether a particular individual's will is indeed good and reflects a true sense of obligations toward others? Kant proposed that a person's will could be considered to be good only if the individual involved was willing to have his/her intent made into a universal law so that everyone in the same situation would not only be free but even encouraged to act in exactly the same way.[45] Kant's question that followed was whether people, making decisions under that rule, would then be satisfied with the world in which they lived if everyone not only was permitted but even encouraged to do exactly the same to all others? This was the first formulation of Kant's universal duty, or Categorical Imperative.

The second formulation of the Categorical Imperative was derived from the first: each person should always treat others as ends, worthy of dignity and respect, and never as a means to his/her own ends.[46] Kant maintained that this second formation had exactly the same meaning as the first, for clearly all individuals would be willing to have everyone else in the world act in exactly this categorically imperative way toward themselves, and treat them as individuals due dignity and respect. The modern version of this universal rule can then be expressed in question format as: "Is the decision or action that I and others in my group or organization are now considering one that treats all others as ends, worthy of dignity and respect, not as means to our own ends, and is it one that we would be willing to see all others free, able, and even encouraged to take?"

The Principle of Combined Rights and Duties
(Pope John XXIII, 1881–1963)

We have not discussed the ethical principles concerning *rights* as one of the ethical principles that contribute to an understanding of the evaluative construct of personal integrity for two reasons. Our first reason is that the moral philosophers who have focused upon rights—Hobbes and Locke were the early ones—essentially concluded that rights had to be embedded in the law, and we have already discussed the existing assumptions and resultant imperfections in the law in chapter 4. Our second reason is that rights and integrity don't seem to fit together all that neatly, except when one has the courage to advocate unpopular rights for other people. Arguing for unpopular rights for one's self, unless that one is a representative of a much larger group, does seem a bit self-seeking, and self-seeking actions are not generally seen as an indication of personal integrity. But, suppose one proposed rights and duties combined.

One modern scholar—and we use the term "scholar" intentionally—did exactly this. That modern scholar was Pope John XXIII, the leader of the Catholic Church from 1958 to 1963.

Pope John XXIII published the encyclical *Pacem im Terris* (Peace on Earth) in 1963.[47] Here there is the traditional emphasis of the Catholic Church upon community, on brotherhood and sisterhood, but also there is more than a trace of an implied rule to "treat each person with dignity and respect" that may have come from Kant, and a very explicit combination of rights and duties that must have come only from himself. The following is our wording of the major points:

1. Any human society, if it is to be well ordered and productive, must be based upon the recognition that every human being is a person with intelligence and free will, and consequently with rights and duties.

2. There is a reciprocity of rights and duties within each person. If a person has a right to life, then he or she has a duty to live it becomingly. If a person has a right to truth, then he or she has a duty to pursue it profoundly.

3. There is a reciprocity of rights and duties between persons. If one person has a right to life, others have a duty to preserve it. If one person has a right to truth, others have a duty to ensure it.

4. Men and women are social by nature, and are meant to live with others and to work for the welfare of all. A recognition of the reciprocal duties

leads to an understanding of spiritual values, and the meaning of truth, justice, charity, and freedom.

These four statements are certainly applicable to everyone, with exceptions for no one, without favoritism for any one, and understandable by all, and thus meet our definition of a legitimate principle, standard, or rule. Again, this is difficult to express in question format, but let us once more make the effort: "Is the decision or action that I and others in my group or organization are now considering one that recognizes the duality of rights and duties? That is, if we have a right to take this decision or action do we have a concurrent duty that goes with that right, and does that duty improve the well-being and rights of others within our society?

The Principle of Distributive Justice (Rawls, 1921–2003)

The contributions of the last two moral philosophers who have contributed to an understanding of the evaluative construct of personal integrity focused upon duties. What do individuals within society, particularly those in managerial positions whose decisions and actions can impact the well-being and rights of others, owe to other members of society? It is unmistakably true that neither John Rawls—the subject of this next-to-the-last segment of chapter 5—nor Robert Nozick—the subject of the last segment—ever mentioned managerial positions or managerial responsibilities, but they both proposed universal, absolute, impartial, and understandable principles, and their derived rules and standards, for people who have the position or power to impact the well-being and rights of others.

It is also unmistakably true that neither John Rawls nor John Nozick ever directly alluded—except perhaps in an obscure paragraph or two—to Immanuel Kant. However, they both offered constraints upon the unlimited duties of Kant, though in each instance with a major advance in that thinking. Many critics over the years have noted that the problem with Kant's first formulation of the universal duty principle, which states that none of us should ever take any action that we would not be willing to see others free or even encouraged to take in roughly similar situations, is that it provides no means for the comparison or relative ranking of alternatives. In Kant's view, a decision or action was either morally right or morally wrong, with no possible gradations between those two extremes. The problem with Kant's second formulation, which states that we should always treat other people as ends, worthy of dignity and respect, and never as means to our own ends, is that it is often hard *not* to treat other people as means to our own ends. Storekeepers, as Adam Smith so clearly declared, are the means to procuring our dinners, customers are the means to earning our livelihoods, and workers are the means of staffing our factories.[48] John Rawls proposed one comparative standard for Kant's "if its right for me it has to be right for everyone" ruling, and he based that measure upon the productive benefits of economic efficiency and the impartial nature of the Social Contract (which he renamed the "Veil of Ignorance").

Prof. Rawls[49] believed that society was an association of free individuals, and that cooperation between those individuals was needed to generate social benefits in the form of marketable goods and services, but that the undoubted benefits of that cooperation were unjustly distributed because some people were excluded from the twin markets for output goods and services and for input material, capital, and labor. These unfortunate "left out" people owned so little material or capital that they had no income from material sales or capital payments, and had so few inherent abilities or educated skills that they were unable to find truly remunerative employment in the input labor markets, and thus had only minimal income to satisfy their needs in the output product markets. Rawls believed that those distributive inequalities were not adequately addressed by the social and political redistributive processes that were an accepted portion of the complete economic efficiency theory.

Rawls suggested that under the conditions of the Social Contract or—as he termed this same concept—the Veil of Ignorance, where people did not know what abilities, skills, or resources they might have, and thus were ignorant of their potential for market-priced earnings to satisfy their market-priced needs, they would make a single and simple agreement. This single and simple agreement would be that inequalities in the distribution of the material and financial benefits of social cooperation would be permitted only as long as it was reasonable to assume that those inequalities would work out to the benefit of all. That is, it would be perfectly all right to pay scientists more than laborers because it would be reasonable to assume that the additional pay would attract more scientists who would invent better products or improved processes that would make life more rewarding for everyone, including the laborers.

Rawls understood that it would be impossible to compute the impacts of all the inequalities in benefit distribution upon the life prospects of all of the people within a society, and so he suggested that all that was needed was to compute the impact upon the "least among us," those with the least education, the least income, and the least skills and abilities, and consequently the ones most likely to be excluded from the normal price-based distribution methods.

The rule he suggested was that people who had been excluded from the normal distribution methods through the lack of marketable monies, materials, or skills had to be benefited in some way, however slight, and should never, under any circumstances, be harmed. This ethical principle, clearly applicable to everyone, avoidable by no one, equitable among everyone, and understandable by all, can be expressed as: "Does the decision or action that I and other members of my group or organization are now considering avoid any negative impact upon the least among us, those with least income, education, wealth, competence, ability, or power so that they can continue to participate, at their current levels, in our output product markets?"

The Principle of Contributive Liberty (Nozick, 1938–2002)

Robert Nozick[50] agreed with John Rawls that society was an association of free individuals, and that cooperation between those individuals was needed to generate social benefits in the form of marketable goods and services, but he argued that this cooperation came about as the result of the free exchanges of those goods and services to satisfy individual desires, and that any exchange that was voluntary had to be just and regarded as proper.

The example he proposed to illustrate that "voluntary exchanges have to be regarded as just and proper" claim involved Wilt Chamberlain, a famed and well-paid basketball player of the era. You could, he explained, set up whatever original set of holdings of property and money you believed to be just and proper among all members of society, but if those same people were willing to pay to see Wilt Chamberlain play basketball, then at the end of a given period of time those holdings would be different, and it would be hard to argue that these new holdings were unjust and improper because all of the exchanges had been voluntary. If all voluntary exchanges were regarded as just and proper, then the Rawls' rule from distributive justice that income inequalities had to work out for the benefit of all, and particularly for the benefit of those who were least able to look after their own self-interests due to a lack of education, income, position, or power, was clearly wrong.

Nozick proposed two new rules that (a) no one should interfere with the voluntary exchanges of other persons; and (b) that no one should interfere with the self-development efforts of those other persons, so that everyone could arrange their own voluntary exchanges to their own best advantage. Liberty, the right to develop skills, was more important than justice, the right to receive benefits, according to Nozick, because self-development led to greater personal abilities and consequently to greater social benefits. The universal principle he proposed, once more applicable to everyone, with exceptions for no one, without favoritism for any one, and understandable by all, in question format could be stated as: "Does the decision or action that I and others in my group or organization are now considering adequately take notice of the rights of everyone, not just the least among us, to develop their skills to the fullest so that they will be better able to arrange their voluntary exchanges as they see most fitting?"

Conclusion to Chapter 5

We have described seven major ethical principles and their derived rules and standards that jointly, as a package, serve as the third evaluative construct for the managerial decisions and actions that benefit some while harming others, or that recognize the rights of some while neglecting the rights of others, *as long as the underlying assumptions are recognized and included.* That is the same conditional acceptance that has been applied to the evaluative constructs of economic efficiency and legal conformity. Given any sense of equity—important in discussing principles derived from moral philosophers—that conditional acceptance clearly should be extended to personal integrity.

Are there underlying assumptions in the various ethical principles, rules, or standards that make up the evaluative construct of personal integrity? Yes, there certainly are, or perhaps we should more accurately say, "Yes, there certainly is." The underlying assumption here is that the people involved in a given situation react similarly to similar perceptions of just treatment. But they don't, or perhaps once again we should more accurately say, "It has never been proven that they do." People come from different economic/social situations and different religious/cultural traditions, and they consequently have different goals, norms, beliefs, and values and thus different standards of personal conduct. They will therefore vary in both their intuitive perceptions of just treatment and their reactions to those perceptions.

Do the assumptions—defects really—that underlie almost equally the evaluative constructs that we have described of economic efficiency, legal conformity, and personal integrity *invalidate* the evaluative processes we have proposed for the decisions and actions of managers that impact, in both positive and negative ways, the well-being and rights of other individuals, groups, organizations, and even societies? *No, certainly not!* The evaluative constructs of economic efficiency, legal conformity, and personal integrity are additive; when used jointly each helps to adjust to the assumptions and/or defects of the others in a sequential reasoning process.

This adjustment happens because economic efficiency, legal conformity, and personal integrity are totally different evaluative constructs with totally different evaluative procedures. Economic efficiency focuses on benefits and harms, as guided by impartial market forces. Legal conformity focuses on rights and duties, as guided by impartial judicial deciders. Personal integrity focuses on constancy and honor, as guided by impartial character traits. When applied sequentially they form a powerful rationale for achieving managerial decisions and actions that can be viewed by the others involved as a right and proper and just *balance* of economic efficiency, legal conformity, and personal integrity. Everyone may not agree with that balance, but at least the standards for the decision are firmly displayed, and thus open to discussion rather than argument.

Our conclusion to this chapter can be divided into two very basic—and unfortunately very lengthy—statements:

1. We admit that the decisions and actions of managers in for-profit, non-profit, and governmental organizations that impact, in both positive and negative ways, the well-being and rights of people associated in some way with those organizations, and that can logically be described as being economically efficient, legally conforming, and personally honorable—honor and integrity do go together—cannot then logically be claimed to be right and just and fair due to the difficulties—which we have perhaps already mentioned far too many times—of precisely defining those terms.

2. But, precise definition is not the important issue in management. The important issue is the *logical perception* of rightness, justness, and fairness among those other people associated with for-profit, non-profit, or governmental organizations, despite their varying goals, norms, beliefs, values, and thus their resultant differing standards of personal conduct. The logical perception of rightness, justness, and fairness among others associated with an organization is the critical issue because those

perceptions have been empirically shown to have major beneficial influences upon the trust, commitment, and cooperative/innovative effort of individuals either employed by or associated with those organizations, and thus upon the performance of those organizations.

Chapter 6, the final chapter in this book, will describe those beneficial influences upon the trust, commitment, and cooperative/innovative efforts of individuals employed by or associated with for-profit, non-profit, or governmental organizations, and upon the efficient, effective, *and honorable* performance of those organizations, together with a sampling of the empirical studies that support those conclusions.

CHAPTER 6

Acknowledging the Results: Trust, Commitment, and Effort

Nucor Corporation is a new and very different type of steel company. Traditional steel companies smelt iron ore, coal, and limestone in blast furnaces to produce cast iron, which is then refined while still in molten form through the use of Bessemer converters to generate steel ingots, which in turn are rolled into steel sheets, plates, bars, and beams for eventual sale to industrial customers. Nucor avoids the blast furnace and Bessemer converter processes; instead this company melts scrap steel in electric arc furnaces, and then directly rolls the output into the needed sheets, plates, bars, and beams. It is a business model that is termed "mini-mill" because the plants are much smaller, with far lower capital investments, and are dispersed throughout the country, with far lower transportation costs for the incoming raw materials and the outgoing finished products. It is a business model that for years was exceedingly successful in the globally competitive steel industry. Company growth rates and profit percentages did level off following the financial services collapse of 2008 and during the subsequent market downturn in the national economy that seems now to just drag on and on, but throughout this awkward period of slow growth and near recession Nucor has been able to maintain a leadership position.

Steel was one of the first of the basic industries to become competitive on a global scale. The raw materials—ore, coal, and limestone—are readily available. The needed technologies—blast furnaces and Bessemer converters—are widely known. The output products—sheets, plates, bars, and beams—are easily sold at reduced prices. Originally, most developing countries lacked the capital to build the expensive plants, but given that their labor costs and environmental restrictions were far lower, the needed capital soon was provided by external investors. The resulting competition drove many of the traditional American and European steel producers into retrenchment, bankruptcy, or both. Nucor Corporation, however, as noted above, not only survived but in 2011 was beginning to prosper again.

> Nucor appears to be back on track Only this time, the well-configured steel and steel products producer—which had fallen in and out of profitability in 2009 and 2010—seems back in the win column on a sustainable basis. Indeed, after a forgettable two years, the opening quarter profit performance—which easily exceeded guidance—should be a harbinger of things to come for the year as a whole.[1]

Financial analysts tend to cite economic factors as the reasons for corporate success, and in this instance they credited the simpler production processes that led to quicker responses to market conditions, wider diversification in product types, and lower investments in capital equipment, but at Nucor there was something else. That "something else" was a highly skilled and totally dedicated workforce that had been described in an earlier article published in *Business Week* during the record-breaking years before the 2008 recession:

> It was about 2:00 p.m. on March 9th when three Nucor Corp. electricians [at different company mills, across the country] got the call from their colleagues at the Hickman (Ark.) plant. It was bad news: Hickman's electric grid had failed. For a mini-mill steelmaker like Nucor, which melts scrap steel in an electric arc furnace to make new steel, there's little that could be worse. The trio immediately dropped what they were doing and headed [for Hickman]. Malcolm McDonald, an electrician from the Decatur (Ala) mill, was in Indiana visiting another facility. He drove down, arriving at 9 o'clock that night. Les Hart and Bryson Trumble, from Nucor's facility in Hertford County, N.C., boarded a plane that landed in Memphis at 11 p.m. Then they drove two hours to the troubled plant.
>
> No supervisor had asked them to make the trip, and no one had to. They went on their own. Camping out in the electrical substation with the Hickman staff, the team worked 20-hour shifts to get the plant up

and running again in three days instead of the anticipated full week. There wasn't any direct financial incentive for them to blow their weekends, no extra money in the next paycheck, but for the company their contribution was huge. Hickman went on to post a first quarter records for tons of steel shipped.[2]

In an industry as rust belt as they come, Nucor employees were—and to our knowledge still are—known widely for their close-knit attitudes and cooperative efforts. These come partially from the company's underdog identity at its beginning. The firm was derided then as an underfunded and unstable start-up by executives at the industry giants that since have largely gone under. But those close-knit attitudes and cooperative efforts come much more directly from an insistence by Kenneth Iverson, the founder, that employees will make exceptional efforts if a company pays them well, treats them with respect, and gives them real power to make on-site operating decisions.

There is no question but that employees at Nucor generally were and to a large extent still are rewarded richly. The basic pay rate for a frontline worker at that company in 2006 when it was cited in the *Business Week* article was just $10.00 per hour, less than half the rate of experienced steel makers at other, much larger companies, but there were bonuses, paid weekly, that were tied to the production of defect-free steel by an employee's entire shift. That bonus could triple the typical take-home check. And, there was an annual distribution based upon corporate profits. Combined, these policies on basic pay, weekly bonus, and yearly distribution resulted in production workers who frequently earned somewhat more than $100,000 per year. Pay rates, weekly bonuses, and annual distributions are no longer publicly reported, but there have been no signs of worker unrest at Nucor so that it can be assumed that they remain at similarly satisfactory levels.

There were, however, penalties that went with the rewards. If a given shift made a bad batch of steel that was shipped to a customer and resulted in problems for and complaints from that customer, then the pay of all members of the shift was docked three times what the bonus would have been. Shift supervisors and plant managers at each mill were also compensated on a similar "penalty three times pay" policy. Their basic pay rates were about 75 percent of the industry average for their positions, but they received annual distributions based upon the return on assets for their own shift or their own plant. In a good year, those annual distributions would equal their basic pay for the full year. This payment policy based upon shift or plant results was adopted, it was said, to ensure a team approach to company problems, and it seemed in another quotation from the 2006 article to have done exactly that. If something broke down in the scrape melting, plate forming, sheet rolling, or product finishing operations at one of the company's mini-mills, the operators of the idled machines would not sit idly, drinking coffee, waiting for the maintenance crew to get things running again. Instead, everyone was expected to head toward the bottleneck, help in the repairs, and jointly get the line running again.

Everyone's pay at Nucor depended on the prompt production of quality steel products. Even the pay rates of the chairman, the president, and the functional—marketing, finance, accounting, and human relations, et cetera—vice presidents were tied tightly to corporate steel shipments, not financial returns, and their pay was limited to a set percentage of the pay of the frontline steel workers. The pay of a CEO at a typical American company averages 400 times that of the hourly paid workers within his or her firm; at Nucor it never went above 14 times.

> "In average to bad years, we earn less than our peers in other companies. That's supposed to teach us that we don't want to be average or bad. We want to be good."[3]

The *Business Week* article stressed the payment amounts and methods at Nucor, but there are other factors that helped then and still help now to create those distinctive attitudes and behaviors. The hierarchy at Nucor was and remains compressed. There were only three levels between the chief executive officer and the frontline workers: production vice president, plant manager, and shift supervisor. Responsibility at Nucor was and remains delegated. Given the narrow hierarchy at the company, workers are expected to solve operating problems on their own, with just the approval of the shift leader. Stability at Nucor is emphasized. Newly hired members of the firm are told that they will have jobs as long as they remain cooperative and productive. Innovation at Nucor is stressed. Employees at all levels are expected to continually recommend improvements in their company's processes through their experiences at work, and in their company's products through their contacts with customers. And lastly, respect at Nucor is guaranteed; there is said to be only one cause for dismissal at Nucor, and that is treating a fellow employee with a lack of consideration and courtesy.

Relationship of Nucor with Managerial Responsibility

The prior chapter ended with the proposal that it was not important whether or not a managerial decision or action that could be described as being a logical balance of economic efficiency, legal conformity, and personal integrity *could be claimed to be right and just and fair.* Those terms, it continued, are simply too difficult to define in complex decisions and actions where some individuals, groups, and organizations will be benefited but others will be harmed, or in which some of those same individuals, groups, and organizations will see their rights recognized while others will see their rights ignored.

The important issue, this ending proposal continued, was whether that logical balance of economic efficiency, legal conformity, and personal integrity *could be perceived to be right and just and fair* by those either employed by or associated with the organization whose managers were making that decision or taking that action. Perceptions are very different from definitions, and for behavioral outcomes they are far more important.

Perceptions of rightness, justness, and fairness vary with the personal conduct standards of individuals, and those personal conduct standards vary with the goals, norms, beliefs, and values of those persons, which in turn are influenced by the cultural/religious traditions and the economic/social situation of each individual. Perceptions of rightness, justness, and fairness are purely personal, and they carry a heavy emotional charge.

This "heavy emotional charge" brings us back to the reason we described the very successful performance of the Nucor Steel Company at the start of this chapter. Here was a company, operating in an industry in which many of the larger firms were failing, and yet meeting both foreign and domestic competition with apparent ease. What competitive advantages did they have? One of those advantages was the use of scrap steel rather than iron ore, limestone, and coke as the primary input materials. This permitted smaller, less capital-intensive plants and closer locations, with quicker deliver times and lower freight costs, both from suppliers and to customers. But any of the larger steel companies could easily have copied this strategy.

The more important part of Nucor's competitive advantage could not so easily be copied. This was the highly productive and obviously committed workforce that jointly and promptly dealt with production problems as they arose, directed by the distributed authority (take charge and get it done) policy, the recognized responsibility (quickly go and help) tradition, and the control and incentive (you'll be evaluated and paid on what you jointly accomplish at your plant and what we together achieve within our company) systems. The overall result was what we term "organizational coherency" throughout Nucor. This is the widespread feeling that "we're all in this together." And, in our view, this came from the strong emotional appeal of the *perceptions of justice in the decisions and actions of the managers at the Nucor Steel Company.*

It has turned out that we are not alone in our belief that the perceptions of justice can impact the attitudes, behaviors, and outputs of persons employed by or associated with a for-profit, non-profit, or governmental organization. This is the central topic of an academic field of study termed "Organizational Justice."

The major theme of Organizational Justice is that the members of an organization who believe that they have been treated in ways they perceive to be just—despite the acknowledged difficulties of defining that oft-used but still imprecise term—tend to respond with: (a) improved *personal attitudes* of managerial trust and organizational commitment; (b) with expanded *group behaviors* of cooperative and innovative effort; and (c) with higher quality—though frequently not higher quantity; we'll explain the reason for this distinction later—*divisional outputs*. The important result, according to numerous empirical studies conducted by researchers within this academic area, is that the members of such an organization tend to draw together with a sense of solidarity extending between the levels, across the functions, and throughout the divisions of for-profit, non-profit, or governmental organizations. There is even some though very limited evidence—due to the massive expansion of the causal factors that have to be first defined, then measured and finally controlled to properly adjust for their impacts as they are brought for the first time into the annual versions of multi-period empirical research projects— that the industry position and financial return of such an organization improve over time.

Our belief is that this sense of solidarity—this belief that "we're all in this together," this condition of *organizational coherency*—has the potential to provide the competitive advantage that individuals, organizations, and societies need in our increasingly competitive, complex, and contentious globalized environment. The following sections will describe the theoretical base and the research findings of this academic construct known as Organizational Justice.

The Theoretical Base of Organizational Justice

Human Behavior in Organizations (HBO) is the broad academic discipline that focuses—as can be easily inferred from its title—upon the decisions, actions, attitudes, behaviors, cultures, and productive outputs of people within for-profit, non-profit, and government organizations. What are the factors that have the potential to influence those decisions, actions, attitudes, behaviors, cultures, and productive outputs in HBO theory? This theory starts with the related claims that people are neither totally rational in their decisions nor fully predictable in their actions, and therefore economic incentives frequently fail to bring about the desired end results. Instead, according to the HBO conceptual framework, individual attitudes, group behaviors, and interdivisional cultures directly affect those end results, and should have equal weight—along with the performance measures and the cash incentives—in our understanding of that important question why some organizations are so very successful, and others most definitely are not.

HBO, in short, looks at the full range of factors—emotional as well as financial—that both contribute to and detract from the desired ends results of effective (achieve set goals) and efficient (conserve scarce resources) organizational performance. Those desired ends of effective and efficient performance, of course, are not limited strictly to managers in business organizations. They are also directly relevant to non-profit and governmental organizations, and to the large professional institutions employing attorneys, doctors, educators, et cetera, which from this point on will be included in our discussions.

This "full range of factors" that may contribute to or detract from the desired ends of effective and efficient organizational performance is obviously huge. Consequently, most of the active scholars within the broad HBO field tend to focus on a special set of those factors for their research projects. One of those special sets is the one with which we are concerned here: Organizational Justice (see figure 6.1).

Organizational Justice is the HBO subdivision that is based upon the *perceptions of justice* of the past, present, and anticipated future treatment of employees within an organization that are held by the employees at all levels (though attention at the start was focused almost entirely upon hourly paid workers) and within all functions (though, again at the start, the manufacturing operations received by far the most attention).

Organizational Justice is a subjective, personal view of justice, based upon experience, rather than a rational determination based upon analysis.

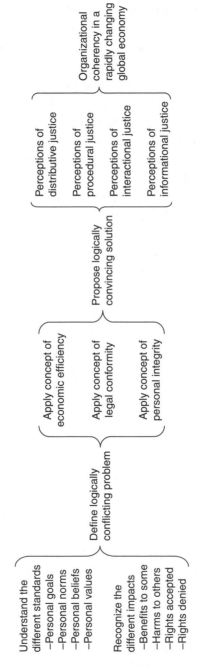

Figure 6.1 Proposed relationship between logical perception of just treatment and organizational coherence.

But, it is a critically important issue when thinking about the nature, the extent, *and now the influence* of managerial responsibility. Why? Because literally hundreds of empirical studies have shown that there are clear relationships between the subjective personal perceptions of justice by the employees of a firm and the positive organizational outcomes at the individual, group, and even divisional levels of that entity.

Specifically, this stream of empirical research has shown that perceived Organizational Justice along a number of dimensions is related to greater organizational coherency—once again, the belief that "we're all in this together"—and that belief can easily be claimed to be essential for success in a rapidly changing and increasingly competitive global environment.

Theoretical Content of Organizational Justice Theory

Our plan is to describe the theoretical content of Organizational Justice in a less than totally strict academic format; that is, without citing each of the multiple scholars who have made significant contributions to the development of each of the four stages of content within this area of study. Instead, we will cite just one author or group of coauthors whose work generally summarizes that content for a given stage in the progression. Before starting this abbreviated discussion, however, let us warn our readers that the term "distributive justice" when used in the HBO literature refers to the perceived fairness of an individual's rate of pay and other remuneration distributions, and not to Rawls' previously described philosophical principle that no one should ever harm the least amongst us. Also before starting let us suggest that Folger and Cropanzano[4] provides an admirable summary of the field for those who might like further information. Now, on to the four ascending stages of the behavioral perceptions of Organizational Justice:

1. *Distributive justice*[5]: is an individual's perception that the *rewards*—the rate of pay and/or selection for promotion—received by that employee were fair in comparison to the payments received and the positions held by other employees of the same firm. The focus during the early development of the full theory of Organizational Justice was much more on pay than on promotion, but it was not just a dollar and cents comparison of that pay. It was an evaluation in an employee's mind of the payment received and position held versus the effort exerted and the contribution provided by that employee, all in comparison to his

or her understanding of the equivalent ratios of the payments, positions, efforts, and contributions for other employees at different levels throughout the firm. A perception of *fairness* in this broad comparison of pay and position was said to be interpreted by the employee as his or her deserved recognition by his or her employer of his or her competitive value and personal worth to the full organization. This is complex subjective thinking, but numerous studies have shown that such analyses, or very close approximations to them, do indeed take place on a regular basis by many if not most employees, and that the perceptions of fairness, given the close association of those beliefs with notions of competitive value and personal worth, have a definite impact upon the attitudes, behaviors, decisions, and actions of those employees.

2. *Procedural justice*[6]: is an individual's perception that the *methods* by which the decisions on individual rewards of pay and promotion of employees were made, all relative to those employees efforts and contributions to the competitive performance of their organization in comparison to the efforts and contributions of others, were themselves fair. These perceptions of fairness were derived from three sources: (a) the openness of all procedures to participation by employees or representatives of those employees; (b) the consistency of all procedures that followed known company policies regarding the persons attending and the information considered; (c) the dependability of all processes, with no uninvited outsiders allowed and no unexpected documents permitted. It has been found that the perceived openness, consistency, and dependability of the decision processes were equally important with the perceived equity of the decision outcomes in determining employee attitudes, behaviors, decisions, and actions.

3. *Interactional justice*[7]: is an individual's perception that the *exchanges* that occurred in the meetings and discussions that were held as part of the procedures during which payment, promotion, and other employment decisions were made were also fair. Fairness in this form originally had a negative connotation: fairness meant that no derogatory comments had been made about a person, and no disrespectful treatments had been accorded to a person. But, it soon gained a more positive understanding that all individuals involved in the process had been treated with definite courtesy and respect. That is, the perception of exchange fairness required that all participants in the procedures not only had an opportunity to speak but also were listened to with a courteous regard for their views. Again, it has been found that the perceived courtesy

and respect of the exchanges, along with the perceived openness, consistency, and dependability of the procedures and the perceived equity of the outcomes, were all important factors in determining employee attitudes, behaviors, decisions, and actions.

4. *Informational justice*: is an individual's perception that the *explanations* provided by the company after the meetings were held, the discussions completed and the decisions made, were themselves fair. Fairness meant informative. Here we are going to break from our earlier policy, and cite a breakthrough article. Sheppard and Lewicki[8] asked a sample of managers within a number of different firms to describe critical incidents of fair and unfair treatment by their superiors during decisions on pay and promotion, and the reasons or standards that brought them to consider those actions as fair or unfair. The distributive perception of their rewards relative to their efforts and contributions in comparison to their understandings of similar ratios for all others throughout the firm was certainly mentioned. The procedural perception of their ability to participate or be represented in the process, and particularly their assurance that there had been consistency in the proceedings, was quickly added. The interactional perception that they and/or their representatives had been treated with courtesy and respect was also stressed. But, most important of all, was their perception of the creditability and adequacy of the explanation. In short, that explanation had to be believable.

We would hope here that readers would note the close similarity between the *logical conviction* required as the end result of our managerial responsibility analysis and the *believable explanation* found as an essential component of the fairness perception in Organizational Justice research. We truly believe that the managerial ability to clearly explain the *logical balance* of economic efficiency, legal conformity, and personal integrity that supports the organizational decisions and actions that impact others is a critical mark of successful leadership within a for-profit, non-profit, or governmental organization.

Why is this leadership? Our view is that this combination of logical reasoning pro-offered by managers and of motivational understanding evidenced by persons employed by the company and/or associated with the company does bring the convinced participants together into a coherent whole whose members are willing to make the effort needed to achieve challenging objectives. Leadership, of course, is another of those frequently used positive terms that are difficult to define, but certainly the ability to bring people together in a common effort to achieve challenging goals should be at least one of the characteristics of that construct. Now, on to the specific findings of Organizational Justice.

The Empirical Findings of Organizational Justice

There have been more than 400 research studies of the relationships between the perceived justice or injustice of the managerial treatment of employees within an organization and the observed individual changes in attitudes, group changes in behaviors, division changes in outputs, and organization changes in performance. Those changes are additive. That is, the individual changes in attitudes influence the group changes in behaviors, and those group changes in behaviors in turn influence the division changes in outputs, and so on. The result is that the research studies at the beginning of that sequence were much easier to conduct and to explain than those at the end because there were far fewer influences to consider and far simpler results to evaluate. But, there have been some very interesting findings to report all along that sequence.

We will report only those findings that were derived from *positive* perceptions of justice among the employees. As we described very briefly in an earlier section, negative perceptions of justice among employees can lead to very negative attitudes, behaviors, and outcomes. From a research point of view, those negative findings at both ends of a study are exceedingly useful because they reinforce the relationships between perceptions of justice and the attitudes and actions of employees. But, we don't think much is learned by showing that if you treat people poorly enough and often enough, over a long enough period of time, on all of the distributional, procedural, interactional, and informational dimensions, then some of those people may respond with the classic "Don't get mad, get even" reaction. That does happen all too frequently, unfortunately, in far too many of our for-profit, non-profit, and governmental organizations.

But, we think much more is learned by demonstrating that if you treat people well enough and frequently enough, over a long enough period of time on those same four fairness dimensions, then they often will react with "What more can I do to help *us* achieve *our* objectives" behavior, and bring subsequent improvements in group cooperation, and intergroup innovation, and divisional production. These latter positive responses are far more important in our view, and we assume in everyone else's view as well, than the negative ones, and so we are going to focus on *positive perceptions and positive reactions*. There are four levels of these positive reactions:

1. *Individual changes in attitudes*[9]: Perceived justice in the distribution of rewards was quickly found to result in greater degrees of pay acceptance, job satisfaction, supervisor approval, et cetera. Once the other input factors of procedural, interactional, and informational justice were added, then the individual changes in attitudes became more focused on organizational issues than on personal matters. Trust in the management, commitment to the company and a willingness to make greater efforts were all stressed in the questionnaires that were returned in the later research studies.

2. *Group changes in behaviors*[10]: Most of the early studies took place in manufacturing companies where work groups assigned to specific tasks were common. Behaviors within those work groups could be observed over time, and it was found that the observed changes in those behaviors could be divided into two types: role based and extra or non-role based. The role-based behaviors were those that were related to the formal operating policies (how a given job was to be done) and the equally formal controls (how the performance of that job was to be measured) and incentives (how the performance of employees who followed those policies and met or exceeded those measures was to be rewarded). The extra or non-role-based behaviors were those that were outside the operating policies and not covered by the control and incentive systems. They included helping group members, fixing group processes, facilitating group interactions, et cetera. Essentially, they improved the functioning of the group.

   The unexpected finding here was that changes in employee perceptions of fairness on any of the four distributional, procedural, interactional, and information dimensions of justice *were found to have little or no influence upon the role-based behaviors and thus it was assumed little impact upon the productive output of the group*. The same jobs continued to be done the same way to meet the existing standards and garner the existing rewards or avoid the existing penalties. But, the non-role behaviors—helping others, making decisions, and even improving processes to make the tasks easier to do and thus lessen the strain or stress on group members—did change, and the employees cited the interactional (the managers treated us with dignity and respect) and informational (the managers fully explained any modifications in policies, controls, or incentives) as the reasons for the their increased willingness to work jointly not only within their own group but between groups. These contrasting outcomes were very disappointing to the researchers because essentially the conclusion of the group changes in behavior studies was that the company wasn't getting any more work done or profit made, but that the employees were having an easier and pleasanter time doing that work in a more cooperative way.

3. *Division changes in outputs*: Organizational Justice researchers soon realized that their studies, which once again had been voluminous in numbers and almost constant in findings, had delivered very little of practical value to for-profit, non-profit, and governmental organizations in terms of output improvements. However, they also recognized that this literature was very rich in implications for such improvements, and so some of the scholars undertook more advanced studies.

These Organizational Justice researchers began to focus on output productivity, which has long been termed the "Holy Grail" of both Organizational Justice and organizational behavior studies. They encountered severe problems here, however. Output improvements may theoretically be claimed to be dependent upon the four forms of justice perceptions by employees at all levels, but they also clearly can be expected to vary with changes in the design of the product, the level of the technology, the investment of capital, the variation in market demand, and the flexibility of the organizational response. It is possible to "control"—that is, to eliminate from the statistical analysis—any influences that might come from changes in these extraneous factors, but the control mechanisms are complex, and require the use of data from other corporate sources that may not be similarly formatted and from other time periods that may not be similarly structured. Lots of adjustments are required, and study adjustments can compromise study findings.

Once again, however, there have been some breakthrough studies. Cowherd and Levine[11] looked at the relationship between output quantity and quality and perceived pay equity between factory-worker wages and senior-executive salaries at 102 different production plants for 42 different business firms. In short, they looked at whether perceived "interclass" injustices would influence worker attitudes, workplace behaviors, and consequence productive outcomes. They found that there was little relationship between perceived pay equity and output quantity, but there was a very strong relationship between pay equity and output quality. Quality, the two authors of the study explained, was a far subtler issue than quantity in measures of productive output; it is much less susceptible to operational control by managers and much more open to discretionary behavior by employees. Bowen, Gilliland, and Folger[12] in an equally important study found that the perceived justice of the full range of management practices at a retail chain (not just pay and position equity) affected not only the individual attitudes and group behaviors of the employees, but that those in turn positively affected the degree of satisfaction and extent of loyalty among customers.

4. *Organizational changes in performance*: Demonstrated improvements in the competitive advantage or financial return of organizations would, of course, be the ideal goal for perception of justice researchers. The problem was that this far more advanced level of their studies brought about an almost exponential expansion of their difficulties. Not only do the researchers have to control for the differences in product designs, technology levels, capital investments, demand variations, and response flexibilities when looking at divisional outputs, but they also have to adjust for differences in economic conditions, industry structures, competitive forces, market trends, organizational resources, social changes, and legal requirements. It proved impossible to adjust for all those factors, and so the research designs had to be greatly simplified yet still meet editorial requirements for scholarly scope. A very few authors have been able to meet those conflicting standards.

Kim and Mauborgne[13] started with the twin assumptions that (1) market, industry, and technical knowledge is the critical resource in a modern economy, and (2) that this critical resource had to be collectively shared to be effectively used in strategic planning for competitive advantage. This sharing, they continued, went beyond the usual contractual arrangement portrayed in principal/agent relationships, and had to be based upon attitudes of managerial trust and organizational commitment. These attitudes of trust and commitment, they then proposed, had to be based upon perceptions of (a) procedural justice (feeling actively involved in all phases of the strategic planning process up to the final decision); (b) informational justice (feeling fully informed about the underlying rationale after the final decision was made by the CEO and/or members of the board of directors); and (c) a third form that they did not name but might have termed evaluational justice (knowing in advance exactly how their performance would be judged throughout the various phases of the planning process).

Those authors interviewed 48 senior executives and strategic planners in 8 participating firms about each company's procedures for strategic planning. Their major finding was that the three forms of justice perception (procedural, informational, and evaluational) were critical to those processes, because collectively they showed that the senior executives recognized the intellectual and emotional worth of the lower-level planners. *Without that recognition of worth, the interviewed planners admitted, they would not have shared their knowledge, but would have saved their best thoughts and most creative ideas for later,* when they were in direct personal contact with the senior people who would at some point in the future determine their salary levels, job assignments, and career opportunities.

Koys[14] followed up on the earlier Bowen, Gilliland, and Folger study that had showed that the perceived justice of managerial practices at a retail chain affected not only the individual attitudes and group behaviors of the employees, but also the service satisfactions and company loyalties of the customers. Koys in his later study looked at how the individual attitudinal changes in job satisfaction and company commitment, and the group behavioral changes in helping and teaching other group members in year "n" at a large restaurant chain then affected single store changes in customer loyalty and unit profitability in year "n+1" at that chain. He found that changes in employee attitudes and behaviors at time "n" indeed were related to changes in customer loyalty and store profitability in year "n+1."

Conclusion to this Chapter

What can we say about the repeated research findings that most employees, many customers, and hopefully more than a few suppliers, distributors, local residents, and fellow citizens respond favorably to perceptions of just treatment in their interactions with managers at for-profit, non-profit, and governmental organizations, and that those favorable responses bring changed attitudes, altered behaviors, improved outputs, and better performances? Intuitively, this proposal makes a great deal of sense. Almost all of us do respond favorably when we find that we have been treated in ways that *we* considered to be right and just and fair.

Empirically, however, these causal relationships are difficult to solidly demonstrate, as shown in figure 6.2. The first problem is the multiplicity

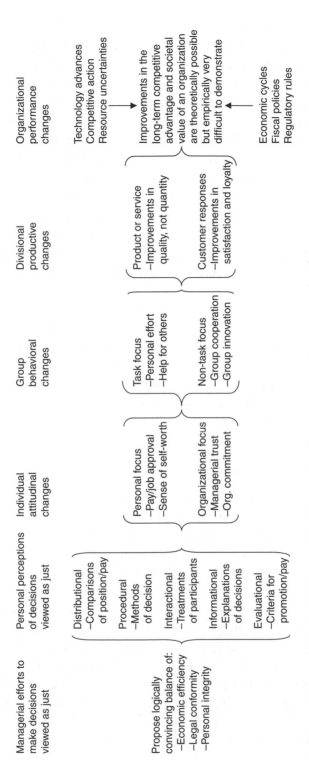

Figure 6.2 Proposed relationship between logical perception of just treatment and organizational performance.

of factors. There are five levels of perception, three stages of change, two different forms of response for each of those stages, all leading up to the final outcome of a long-term competitive advantage, with measurement problems for all of those intermediate levels, stages, and forms and—particularly—for that last final outcome. The second problem is that these levels of perception and the stages of individual, group, and divisional change, all with their different forms, are sequentially interrelated in patterns that vary with the difficulty of the tasks that are required and the nature of the competitive advantage that is sought. And lastly, the third problem is that the final outcome is substantially: (a) influenced by industry-wide technological advances, competitive actions, and supply shortages; and (b) determined by national economic cycles, fiscal policies, and regulatory alterations. Both the "a" influences and "b" conditions, of course, are almost entirely beyond the control of the managers within a single organization.

We have attempted to show, in figure 6.2, the complex pattern of relationships, influences, and policies that make meaningful empirical research into the validity of extended Organizational Justice claims that perceptions of just treatment by the members of organizations do improve the strategic and operational performance outcomes of organizations so difficult to establish, but so sensible to attempt. We sincerely hope that this book will encourage that attempt.

Conclusion to the Book

Our competitive global economy, our advancing technological capabilities, and our contentious national societies have jointly made our world a confusing and difficult place. Changes are constant along many dimensions, both new and old. Reactions to those changes, in for-profit, non-profit, and governmental organizations, are both difficult and delayed. The reassuring notion of a comparative advantage for countries used to last for centuries, but now winds down after maybe 50 years. The equally reassuring idea for a competitive advantage for companies used to last for decades, but now can be obliterated within just a few years.

Our conclusion to this book is that it is the responsibility of managers within for-profit, non-profit, and governmental organizations—and of professionals within their dedicated organizations as well—to deal successfully with that confusion and change, with that difficulty and delay, and particularly with that continuing need for a comparative and/or competitive advantage. Countries and companies alike need something that sets themselves apart as something both valuable and valued, something worthy of trust, dedication, and effort.

But how does one achieve that trust, dedication, and effort? To speak in blunt yet obvious terms one cannot buy it—it is not capital based—and one cannot systematize it—it is not technology based. It is people based. And, maybe what is needed for those people to make more effective (achieve set goals) and more efficient (conserve scarce resources) use of that monetary capital and technological competence is a feeling among all those people—the employees at all levels, the investors of all types, the participants in all joint ventures, and the contributors to all value chains—that "we're all in this together; we can only succeed and grow as a unit."

The problem is that people are more divided now than they have ever been. They are divided on the global level by nation, by language, by culture, and by governments. They are divided on the social level by income, by education, by background, by class, and by contacts. They are divided on the organizational level by division, by position, by function, and by assignments. And lastly, they are divided on the group level by their personal goals, norms, beliefs, values, and behavioral standards.

How should managers at for-profit, non-profit, and governmental organizations, and the professionals who work for and/or with those organizations, attempt to draw these separated individuals together into a "we're all in this together, we'll succeed and grow as a unit" effort? Maybe—and this will be the next to the last "maybe" in this book—it is to attempt to provide a logically convincing explanation of their decisions and actions that may benefit some individuals, groups, and organizations while harming others, or that may recognize the rights of some of those individuals, groups, and organizations while ignoring the rights of others.

Such a logically convincing explanation can be achieved only by balancing the evaluative constructs of economic efficiency, legal conformity, and personal integrity. These constructs truly are universal (applicable to everyone), absolute (with exceptions for no one), impartial (without favoritism for any one), and basic (understandable by all). There are assumptions and/or defects in each construct that have to be recognized. But taken together, a rational balance of these evaluative constructs in decisions and actions that impact others comes as close as is possible to a perception of justice among all of those impacted by a given managerial decision or action. *And maybe—and this truly is that last "maybe" in our book—a perception of just treatment is the most basic motivating force in all of human behavior.*

Justice—as we have already explained perhaps far too many times—is neither a definable concept nor an achievable goal. But our argument is that when we look at justice as a process rather than an outcome, and if we think of that process as one leading to the single goal of coherency within our organizations and within our societies, *given the understanding that we can't have one over the long-term without the other,* then we do have a readily measurable end result based upon attitudes and behaviors, which will help in the definition of both leadership and justice. *For, in our view, leadership is the achievement of the perception of justice.*

Our last statement within this book is that, after the introduction, we have devoted separate chapters to economic efficiency, legal conformity, personal integrity, and organizational coherency. We hope that readers have noticed, as we moved from one chapter to the next, that we were not going to a different subject, we were just moving to a different discipline. Economics, law, integrity, and behavior should, in our view, be considered jointly. It is unfortunate that they are studied so separately.

Notes

Preface

1. Financial Crisis Inquiry Commission, *The Financial Crisis Inquiry Report: Final Report of the National Commission on the Causes of the Financial and Economic Crisis in the United States* (Washington, DC: US Government Printing Office, 2011), 22.

1   Defining the Problem

1. National Commission on the BP Deepwater Horizon Oil Spill and Offshore Drilling, *Deepwater: The Gulf Oil Disaster and the Future of Offshore Drilling* (Washington, DC: US Government Printing Office, 2011), 4.
2. Ibid., 44.
3. Ibid., 46.
4. Ibid., 3.
5. Ibid., 2.
6. Ibid., 91.
7. Ibid., 4. We believe that the term "coming out of the hole" refers to the completion of the process of preparing an oil well for closure.
8. National Commission, *Deepwater*, 7.
9. Ibid., 8.
10. Ibid., 9.
11. Ibid., 9.
12. Ibid., 11.
13. Ibid., 23.
14. "In Report on Gulf Spill, BP Sheds Some Light and Casts Much Blame," *New York Times*, September 9, 2010: A14.
15. National Commission, *Deepwater*, 95.
16. Ibid., 97.

17. Ibid., 116. It is not clear to us what the BP engineer meant by the phrase "stuck above wellhead." Our interpretation, given the context, is "have to wait beyond the expected closure date."
18. National Commission, *Deepwater*, 99–100.
19. Ibid., 105–109.
20. Ibid., l6.
21. Ibid., 4 and 103.
22. Ibid., 90.

2 Proposing the Solution

1. *Merriam-Webster Dictionary* (Springfield, MA: Merriam-Webster, Inc., 1997) 425.
2. Frank Knight, *Risk, Uncertainty and Profit* (Boston and New York: Houghton Mifflin Co., 1921), 19–20.

3 Applying the Evaluative Construct of Economic Efficiency

1. Financial Crisis Inquiry Commission, *The Financial Crisis Inquiry Report: Final Report of the National Commission on the Causes of the Financial and Economic Crisis in the United States* (Washington, DC: US Government Printing Office, 2011).
2. Ibid., xv–xvi.
3. Ibid., 23.
4. Ibid., 6.
5. Ibid., 10.
6. Ibid., 5.
7. Ibid., 5–6.
8. Ibid., 4.
9. Ibid., 7.
10. Ibid., xxiii.
11. Ibid.
12. Ibid.
13. Ibid., 7.
14. Permanent Subcommittee on Investigations, United States Senate, *Wall Street and the Financial Crisis: Anatomy of a Financial Collapse* (Washington, DC: US Government Printing Office, 2011).
15. Ibid., 8.
16. Ibid., 6.
17. Ibid.
18. Financial Crisis Inquiry Commission, *The Financial Crisis Inquiry Report*, 6.
19. Ibid., 22.

20. Ibid., xix.

21. Ibid., 3.

22. Ibid., 10.

23. Ibid.

24. Ibid., 13.

25. Ibid., 14–15.

26. Ibid., 15–16.

27. Ibid., 16.

28. Ibid., 17.

29. Ibid.

30. Ibid.

31. Ibid., 19.

32. Ibid.

33. "In Report on Gulf Spill, BP Sheds Some Light and Casts Much Blame," *New York Times*, September 9, 2010, A14.

34. Financial Crisis Inquiry Commission, *The Financial Crisis Inquiry Report*, xv–xvi.

35. Ibid., xv.

36. Ibid.

4 Applying the Evaluative Construct of Legal Conformity

1. United States Senate Permanent Subcommittee on Investigations, *Staff Report on Tax Haven Banks and U.S. Tax Compliance* (Washington, DC: US Government Printing Office, July 17, 2008), 2.

2. Ibid., 2.

3. Ibid., 9.

4. Ibid., 1.

5. Ibid., 10.

6. Ibid., 54.

7. Ibid., 10.

8. United States Permanent Subcommittee on Investigations, *Statement of Senator Carl Levin on Tax Haven Banks and U.S. Tax Compliance: Obtaining the Names of U.S. Citizens with Swiss Accounts* (Washington, DC: US Government Printing Office, March 14, 2009), 3.

9. Ibid., 2.

10. United States Permanent Subcommittee on Investigations, *Staff Report on Tax Haven Banks*, 92.

11. Ibid., 91.

12. Ibid., 93.

13. Ibid.

14. Ibid., 95.

15. Ibid., 100.

16. United States Senate Committee on Homeland Security and Government Affairs (US SCHS&GA), *U.S. Tax Shelter Industry: The Role of Accountants, Lawyers and Financial Professionals* (Washington, DC: US Government Printing Office, November 18, 2003).

17. "Nine Are Charged in KPMG Case on Tax Shelters," *Wall Street Journal*, August 30, 2005.

18. "8 Former Partners of KPMG Are Indicted," *New York Times*, August 30, 2005.

19. "KPMG Trial Pared in Scope, Nears End after Stormy Prologue," *Wall Street Journal*, October 12, 2007.

20. US SCHS&GA, *U.S. Tax Shelter Industry*, 4.

21. Ibid., 5–9.

22. *Concise Oxford Dictionary of Quotations*, 5th ed., Susan Radcliffe, ed. (Oxford and New York: Oxford University Press, 2008).

23. *Oxford Dictionary of Quotations*, "Misquotations Section," Elizabeth Knowles, ed. (Oxford and New York: Oxford University Press, 2009), www.oxfordreferencel.com.

24. "Credit Card Holders Could Have More Say in Court," Prepared by the Associated Press for the *New York Times*, July 22, 2009, http://aponline/2009/-07/22AP.

25. "City Law Firm's Immigration Video Sparks an Intense Firestorm," *Pittsburgh Post Gazette*, June 22, 2007.

26. Deborah Rhode, *In the Interests of Justice: Reforming the Legal Profession* (Oxford and New York: Oxford University Press, 2000) 2.

27. Ibid., 82.

28. Ibid., 55–56.

29. Mary Ann Glendon, *A Nation Under Lawyers: How the Crisis in the Legal Profession Is Transforming American Society* (Cambridge, MA: Harvard University Press, 1994) 2.

30. Ibid., 29.

31. Ibid., 36.

32. Ibid., 31.

33. Roscoe Pound, "Law in Books and Law in Action," 44 *American Law Review* Vol. 12, 1910, 12–36.

34. Marc Galantier, "Why the Haves Come Out Ahead: Speculations on the Limits of Legal Change," *Law and Society Review* Vol. 9, 1976, 95–160.

35. William Gaddis, *A Frolic of His Own* (New York: Poseidon Press, 1994) 11.

36. Galantier, "Why the Haves Come Out Ahead," 1 and Rhode, *In the Interests of Justice,* 56.

37. Richard Zitrin and Carol Langford, *The Moral Compass of the American Lawyer: Trust, Justice, Power and Greed* (New York: Ballentine Books, 1999) 55.

5   Applying the Evaluative Construct of Personal Integrity

1. "RC2's Train Wreck," *New York Times*, June 19, 2007.
2. "As More Toys Are Recalled, Trail Ends in China," *New York Times*, June 19, 2007.
3. Richard Rorty, "Is Philosophy Relevant to Applied Ethics," *Business Ethics Quarterly*, 2006, 371.
4. Jeremy Bentham, *A Fragment on Government and an Introduction to the Principles of Morals and Legislation* (Oxford: Basil Blackwell, 1948).
5. John Stuart Mill, *Utilitarianism* (Indianapolis, IN: The Bobbs-Merrill Company, 1987).
6. Adam Smith, *An Inquiry into the Nature and Causes of the Wealth of Nations*, R. H. Campbell and A. S. Skinner, eds. Glasgow Edition of the Works and Correspondence of Adam Smith. (Oxford: Oxford University Press, 1976).
7. Thomas Hobbes, *Leviathan* (New Jersey: Cambridge University Press, 1991).
8. John Locke, *Two Treatise of Government* (New Jersey: Cambridge University Press, 1960).
9. Robin Waterfield, *The First Philosophers: The Pre-Socratics and Sophists* (Oxford: Oxford University Press, 2000), 213.
10. Brad Inwood and L. P. Gerson, *Hellenistic Philosophy*, Vol. II (Indianapolis: Hackett Publishing Inc., 1997), 102.
11. G. M. A. Grube and C. D. C. Reeve, *Plato's Republic* (Indianapolis: Hackett Publishing, Inc. 1992), 35–36.
12. Aristotle, *Aristotle's Nicomachean Ethics*, Robert C. Bartle and Susan D. Collins, Trans. (Chicago: University of Chicago Press, 2011).
13. Ibid., 5.
14. Ibid., 6.
15. Ibid., 6–7.
16. Ibid., 16.
17. Ibid., 23.
18. Ibid., 223–224.
19. Ibid., 224.
20. Ibid., 2.
21. Ibid., 3.
22. Grube and Reeve, *Plato's Republic*, 109–112.
23. Aristotle, *Aristotle's Nicomachean Ethics*, 46.
24. Ibid., 55–68.
25. Ibid., 69–80.
26. Ibid., 81–85.
27. Ibid., 87.
28. Ibid., 92.
29. Ibid.

30. Ibid.

31. Ibid., 95.

32. Ibid., 99.

33. Greg M. Epstein, *Good without God: What a Billion Nonreligious People Do Believe* (New York: HarperCollins, 2010), 115.

34. "Udanavarga 5:18," *Udanavarga: A Collection of Verses from the Buddhist Canon*, W. Woodville Rockhill, Trans. (London: Kegan, Paul, Trench, Trubner and Co., 1982), 27.

35. "Mathew 7:12," *Holy Bible: Containing the Old and New Testaments*, Vol. 4 (New York: American Bible Association, 1859), 883.

36. "Luke 6:31," *Holy Bible*, 939.

37. "Analytics 5:23," *The Four Books: Confucian Analytics, The Great Learning, the Doctrine of the Mean and the Works of Mencius*, James Legge, Trans. (China: The Commercial Press, not dated), 229.

38. *Encyclopedia of Canonical Hadith*, G. H. A. Juynboll, Trans. (Leiden, The Netherlands; Boston: Brill, 2007), 477.

39. "Shabbat 31a," *The Talmud*, H. Palano, Trans. (Philadelphia: The Book Tree, 2003), 230.

40. Aristotle, *Aristotle's Nicomachean Ethics*, 99.

41. *Tai-Shang Kan-Ying P'ien: Treatise of the Exalted One on Repose and Retribution*, Teitaro Suzuki and Paul Carus, Trans. (Chicago: The Open Court Publishing Company, 1906), 53.

42. D. W. Robertson, *Saint Augustine: On Christian Doctrine* (New York: The Liberal Arts Press, 1987), 24.

43. St. Thomas Aquinas, *Summa Contra Gentiles,* Book III Part II, Vernon J. Bourke, Trans. (New York: Hanover House, 1957), 159.

44. Immanuel Kant, *Groundwork for the Metaphysics of Morals*, Lawrence Pasternack, ed. (London: Routledge Press, 2002), 1.

45. Ibid., 57.

46. Ibid.

47. Pope John XXIII, *Pacem im Terris*, Henry Waterhouse, ed. (London: The Catholic Truth Society, 1980), 3.

48. Smith, *An Inquiry into the Nature*, 19.

49. John Rawls, *A Theory of Justice*, Rev. Ed. (Cambridge, MA: Harvard University Press, 1999).

50. Robert Nozick, *Anarchy, State and Utopia* (New York: Basic Books, 1974).

6 Acknowledging the Results: Trust, Commitment, and Effort

1. "Nucor, Inc.," *Value Line Investment Survey* (Newark, NJ: Value Line Publishing, LLC, June 17, 2011), 746.

2. "The Art of Motivation: What You Can Learn from a Company That Treats Workers Like Owners. Inside the Surprising Performance Culture of Steelmaker Nucor," *Business Week*, May 1, 2006, 56–58.

3. Ibid., 57.

4. Robert Folger and Russel Cropanzano, *Organizational Justice and Human Resource Management* (Thousand Oaks, CA: Sage Publications, 1998).

5. J. Stacy Adams, "Inequity in Social Exchange," *Advances in Experimental Social Psychology*, Vol. II, L. Berkowitz, ed. (New York: Academic Press, 1965), 167–299.

6. John Thibault and Laurens Walker, *Procedural Justice: A Psychological Analysis* (Hillsdale, NJ: Lawrence Erlbaum Press, 1975).

7. Robert J. Bies, "Interactional (In)justice: The Sacred and Profane," *Advances in Organizational Justice*, J. Greenberg and R. Cropanzano, eds. (Stanford, CA: Stanford University Press, 1986), 89–118.

8. Blair H. Sheppard and Roy J. Lewicki, "Towards General Principles of Managerial Fairness," *Social Justice Research* Vol. I, 1987, 161–176.

9. Thomas R. Tyler and Robert J. Bies, "Beyond Formal Procedures: The Interpersonal Context of Procedural Justice," in *Advances in Applied Social Psychology: Business Settings*, James Carroll, ed. (Hillsdale, NJ: Lawrence Erlbaum Press, 1989), 77–98.

10. Denis W. Organ, *Organizational Citizenship Behavior: The Good Soldier Syndrome* (Lexington, MA: Lexington Books, 1988).

11. Douglas E. Cowherd and David I. Levine, "Product Quality and Pay Equity between Lower-Level Employees and Top Management: An Investigation of Distributive Justice Theory," *Administrative Science Quarterly* 37, 1991, 302–320.

12. David E. Bowen, Stephen W. Gilliland, and Russell Folger, "HRM and Service Fairness: How Being Fair with Employees Spills Over to Customers," *Organizational Dynamics* Vol. 27, 1999, 89–118.

13. W. Chan Kim and Renee Mauborgne, "Procedural Justice, Strategic Decision Making and the Knowledge Economy," *Strategic Management Journal* Vol. 19, 1998, 323–338.

14. Daniel J. Koys, "The Effects of Employee Satisfaction, Organizational Citizenship Behavior and Turnover on Organizational Effectiveness," *Personnel Psychology* Vol. 54, 2001, 101–124.

Bibliography

Adams, J. Stacy. "Inequity in Social Exchange." In *Advances in Experimental Social Psychology*, L. Berkowitz, ed., Vol. 1. New York: Academic Press, 1965.

Aristotle. *Aristotle's Nicomachean Ethics*. Robert C. Bartle and Susan D. Collins, trans. Chicago, IL: University of Chicago Press, 2011.

Aquinas, St. Thomas. *Summa Contra Gentiles,* Book III Part II. Vernon J. Bourke, trans. New York: Hanover House, 1957.

Bentham, Jeremy. *A Fragment on Government and an Introduction to the Principles of Morals and Legislation.* Oxford: Basil Blackwell, 1948.

Bies, Robert J. "Interactional (In)justice: The Sacred and Profane." In *Advances in Organizational Justice.* J. Greenberg and R. Cropanzano, eds. Palo Alto, CA: Stanford University Press, 1986.

Bowen, David E., Steven W.Gilliland, and Russell Folger. "HRM and Service Fairness: How Being Fair with Employees Spills Over to Customers." *Organizational Dynamics* Vol. 27, 1999.

Concise Oxford Dictionary of Quotations, 5th ed. Susan Radcliffe, ed. Oxford and New York: Oxford University Press, 2008.

Cowherd, Douglas E. and David I. Levine. "Product Quality and Pay Equity between Lower-Level Employees and Top Management: An Investigation of Distributive Justice Theory." *Administrative Science Quarterly* Vol. 37, 1992.

Encyclopedia of Canonical Hadith. G. H. A. Juynboll, trans. Leiden, The Netherlands; Boston: Brill, 2007.

Financial Crisis InquiryCommission. *The Financial Crisis Inquiry Report: Final Report of the National Commission on the Causes of the Financial and Economic Crisis in the United States.* Washington, DC: US Government Printing Office, 2011.

Folger, Robert and Russell Cropanzano. *Organizational Justice and Human Resource Management.* Thousand Oaks, CA: Sage Publications, 1998.

Four Books: The Confucian Analytics, The Great Learning, The Doctrine of the Mean and the Works of Mencius. James Legge, trans. and ed. China: The Commercial Press, not dated.

Friedman, Milton and Rose D. Friedman. *Capitalism and Freedom.* Chicago, IL: University of Chicago Press, 1982.

Gaddis, William. *A Frolic of His Own.* New York: Poseidon Press, 1994.

Galantier, Marc. "Why the Haves Come Out Ahead: Speculations on the Limits of Legal Change." *Law and Society Review* Vol. 9:1, 1995, pp. 95–160.

Glendon, Mary E. *A Nation Under Lawyers: How the Crisis in the Legal Profession Is Transforming American Society.* Cambridge, Ma: Harvard University Press, 1994.

Grube, G. M. A and C. D. C. Reeve. *Plato Republic.* Indianapolis, IN: Hackett Publishing, Inc., 1992.

Hobbes, Thomas. *Leviathan.* New Jersey: Cambridge University Press, 1991.

Inwood, Brad and L. P. Gerson. *Hellenistic Philosophy*, Vol. II. Indianapolis, IN: Hackett Publishing, Inc., 1997.

Kant, Immanuel. *Groundwork for the Metaphysics of Morals.* Lawrence Pasternack, ed. London: Routledge, 2002.

Kim, W. Chan and Renee Mauborgne. "Procedural Justice, Strategic Decision Making and the Knowledge Economy." *Strategic Management Journal* Vol. 19, 1998.

Knight, Frank. *Risk, Uncertainty and Profit.* Boston and New York: Houghton Mifflin Co., 1921.

Koys, Daniel J. "The Effects of Employee Satisfaction, Organizational Citizenship Behavior and Turnover on Organizational Effectiveness." *Personnel Psychology* Vol. 54, 2001.

Locke, John. *Two Treatise of Government.* New Jersey: Cambridge University Press, 1960.

Luke. *The Holy Bible, New Revised Standard Version.* New York: American Bible Society, 1987.

Mathew. *The Holy Bible, New Revised Standard Version.* New York: American Bible Society, 1987.

Merriam-Webster Dictionary. Springfield, MA: Merriam-Webster, Inc. 1997.

Mill, John Stuart. *Utilitarianism.* Indianapolis, IN: The Bobbs-Merrill Company, 1987.

National Commission on the BP Deepwater Horizon Oil Spill and Offshore Drilling. *Deepwater: The Gulf Oil Disaster and the Future of Offshore Drilling.* Washington, DC: US Government Printing Office, 2011.

Nozick, Robert. *Anarchy, State and Utopia.* New York: Basic Books, 1974.

Organ, D. W. *Organizational Citizenship Behavior: The Good Soldier Syndrome.* Lexington, MA: Lexington Books, 1988.

Oxford Dictionary of Quotations. "Misquotations Section." Elizabeth Knowles, ed. Oxford and New York: Oxford University Press, 2009, www.oxfordreference.com/views/ENTRY.html/subview=Main&entry=t115e2306

Permanent Subcommittee on Investigations, United States Senate. *Wall Street and the Financial Crisis: Anatomy of a Financial Collapse.* Washington, DC: US Government Printing Office, 2011.

Pope John XXIII. *Pacem im Terris.* Henry Waterhouse, ed. London: The Catholic Truth Society, 1980.

Pound, Roscoe. "Law in Books and Law in Action." 44 *American Law Review* Vol. 12, 1910, pp. 12–36.

Rawls, John. *A Theory of Justice.* Rev. ed. Cambridge, MA: Harvard University Press, 1999.

Rhode, Deborah E. *In the Interests of Justice: Reforming the Legal Profession.* Oxford and New York: Oxford University Press, 2000.

Robertson, D. W. *Saint Augustine: On Christian Doctrine.* New York: The Liberal Arts Press, 1987.

Rorty, Richard. "Is Philosophy Relevant to Applied Ethics." *Business Ethics Quarterly* Vol. 16, July 2006.

Sheppard, Blair H. and Roy J. Lewicki. "Towards General Principles of Managerial Fairness." *Social Justice Research* Vol. 1, 1987.

Smith, Adam. *An Inquiry into the Nature and Causes of the Wealth of Nations.* R. H. Campbell and A. S. Skinner, eds. Glasgow Edition of the Works and Correspondence of Adam Smith, Oxford: Oxford University Press, 1976.

Tai-Shang Kan-Ying P'ien: Treatise of the Exalted One on Repose and Retribution. Teitaro Suzuki and Paul Carus, trans. Chicago: The Open Court Publishing Company, 1906.

Talmud. H. Palano, trans. Philadelphia: The Book Tree, 2003.

Thibault, John and Laurens Walker. *Procedural Justice: A Psychological Analysis.* Hillsdale, NJ: Lawrence Erlbaum Press, 1975.

Tyler, Thomas R. and Robert J. Bies. "Beyond Formal Procedures: The Interpersonal Context of Procedural Justice." In *Advances in Applied Social Psychology: Business Settings.* James Carroll, ed. Hillsdale, NJ: Lawrence Erlbaum Press, 1989.

Udanavarga: A Collection of Verses from the Buddhist Canon. W. Woodville Rockhill, trans. London: Kegan, Paul, Trench, Trubner and Co., 1892.

United States Senate Committee on Homeland Security and Governmental Affairs. *U.S. Tax Shelter Industry: The Role of Accountants, Lawyers and Financial Professionals.* Washington, DC: US Government Printing Office, November 18, 2003.

United States Senate Permanent Subcommittee on Investigations. *Staff Report on Tax Haven Banks and U.S. Tax Compliance.* Washington, DC: US Government Printing Office, July 17, 2008.

United States Senate Permanent Subcommittee on Investigations. *Statement of Senator Carl Levin* on *Tax Haven Banks and U.S. Tax Compliance: Obtaining the Names of U.S. Clients with Swiss Accounts.* Washington, DC: US Government Printing Office, March 4, 2009.

Waterfield, Robin. *The First Philosophers: The Pre-Socratics and Sophists*. Oxford: Oxford University Press, 2000.

Zitrin, Richard and Carol M.Langford. *The Moral Compass of the American Lawyer: Trust, Justice, Power and Greed*. New York: Ballentine Books, 1999.

Index

Note: Page locators in italics indicate figures.